Haunted
Colorado

D1528795

Haunted Colorado

Ghosts and Strange Phenomena of the Centennial State

Charles A. Stansfield Jr.

Illustrations by Marc Radle

STACKPOLE BOOKS

To my nearest and dearest—
Diane, Wayne, Paul, Beth, Jordan, Aidan
and Bryce—with all my love

Published by
STACKPOLE BOOKS
5067 Ritter Road
Mechanicsburg, PA 17055
www.stackpolebooks.com

Printed in the United States of America

10 9 8 7 6 5 4 3 2 1

FIRST EDITION

Cover design by Tessa J. Sweigert

Library of Congress Cataloging-in-Publication Data

Stansfield, Charles A.
  Haunted Colorado : ghosts and strange phenomena of the centennial state / Charles A. Stansfield, Jr. — 1st ed.
      p. cm.
  Includes bibliographical references.
  ISBN-13: 978-0-8117-0855-5 (pbk.)
  ISBN-10: 0-8117-0855-1 (pbk.)
  1. Ghosts—Colorado. 2. Haunted places—Colorado. I. Title.
  BF1472.U6.S724 2011
  133.109788—dc22
                              2011016351

Contents

Contents

Introduction

THE WORLD CAN BE A SCARY PLACE, REGARDLESS OF WHETHER OR NOT you are a firm believer in things supernatural. Daily television program listings show a popular fascination with ghosts, demons, witches, vampires, and monsters of all descriptions. Do we want to be scared? Do we enjoy a bit of terror while in the comfortable security of our own homes?

Are you a true believer in the supernatural or a confirmed skeptic, secure in your rational conviction that there is not such a phenomenon as ghosts? Partisans of both of these extremes may together add up to a numerical majority, with the balance of the population open-minded skeptics—those who believe that ghosts probably don't exist, but that it would be interesting if they did.

Whether skeptic, believer, or unconvinced but open-minded, all can enjoy a good story. Tales of the supernatural are not only entertaining; they might provide an avenue to explore our deep feelings about such weighty topics as the nature of life and death. We need to ponder such basic concerns in ways that mask the profoundly emotional nature of the topics. We need to keep our cool, at least outwardly.

Consider how the celebration of Halloween has changed in the last few decades. The original pagan festival of the dead, known as All Hallows' Eve, marked the end of the harvest season and the onset of winter. The veil of mystery that separates the worlds of the living and the dead was believed to be at its most transparent at this time. Communication between the living and dead became much easier, and on the eve of the holiday, the spirits of the dead roamed the land of the living. The ancient Celts, and their modern spiritual descendants, believed that the devil and witches could most effectively exercise their special powers on All Hallows' Eve.

By the early twentieth century, much of the serious nature of the holiday had disappeared under a party atmosphere. It became essentially a kids' holiday, an excuse to dress up in costumes and gorge on candy for one evening. Now, it has been transformed into an occasion for decorating houses and lawns. Fake tombstones with witty epitaphs sprout from suburban lawns. Imitation cobwebs and miniature ghosts festoon trees. Perhaps the gentle mocking of death on Halloween acts as a safety valve to diminish our fears about death. We can reduce the fearsome mysteries surrounding death by dressing up as ghosts.

Interest in the supernatural is universal across both space and time. Every human society that now exists or has ever existed has traditions of ghosts, witches, demons, and monsters. Sometimes the details of these stories are amazingly similar. For example, as fans of Dracula movies know, Eastern European tales about vampires feature what is known as "shape-shifting." Allegedly, vampires can transform themselves from human form into wolves or bats. More than seven thousand miles away, America's largest tribe, the Navajo, believe that witches can morph from human form into wolves or owls. Can it be pure coincidence that people so far apart and so different in cultures, religions, and languages just happen to have almost identical ancient legends?

Belief in witchcraft was so strong in Europe four and five centuries ago that scores of thousands of people were either hanged or burned alive for being convicted of witchcraft. In England alone, thirty thousand people were executed because their neighbors thought they were witches. Housecats were thought to be "familiars," the feline henchmen of human witches. In an orgy of senseless violence, hundreds of thousands of cats were killed throughout Europe. Ironically, this led to a huge expansion of the rat population—rats that helped spread the dreaded Black Death, or bubonic plague.

Many people who would firmly deny a belief in witchcraft nonetheless have superstitions that influence their thinking and behavior. For example, many believe that they have lucky numbers. There are those who customarily wear a lucky item of clothing or jewelry. If you believe in luck, then you believe that unseen forces of good or evil can shape events or direct our lives, at least to some degree.

Whether or not you believe in ghosts and other supernatural phenomena, you can still be intrigued, entertained, amused, and yes, frightened by such stories. You are about to discover Colorado's dark side, its hidden world of ghosts, demons, witches, and monsters.

Many ghosts are historic in one of several senses. They may be the product of a famous incident or disaster, such as a frontier massacre. Some apparitions appear to be the phantoms of famous or infamous Colorado residents from the past, including the ghosts of Butch Cassidy and the Sundance Kid, movie star Douglas Fairbanks, boxer Jack Dempsey, and *Titanic* survivor Molly Brown. The spirit of Buffalo Bill also makes an appearance.

The ghosts are geographic, in two senses. Many phantoms reflect the cultural, economic, and physical geography of Colorado. Many ghost stories set in the Rocky Mountains, for example, feature gold miners, mining towns, and famous resort hotels. Most ghosts are highly territorial. Their haunts are often tightly circumscribed—a room in a building, a corner of a basement, and so on.

The stories have been grouped into five general regions: Metropolitan Denver, Northern Plains, Rocky Mountains, Southern Plains, and Western Plateaus and Deserts. Enjoy your tour of the spooky side of the Centennial State. Keep the doors locked and the lights on. Nobody knows for sure if all, or any, of these stories are true.

Metropolitan Denver

THE METROPOLITAN DENVER AREA IS THE SMALLEST OF THE FIVE REGIONS of Colorado in area, but the largest in population. This region centers on the state capital and largest city and includes the area from Broomfield and Brighton in the north to Aurora and Centennial to the south.

In this compact region, you will encounter the spirits of Buffalo Bill and the Unsinkable Molly Brown. There is also a young woman who suspects that her pet fish might be psychic and twins who discover they have a supernatural bond. Saddest of all is the ghost in a hotel grieving about her future husband's tragic end.

It's Good to Be a Twin

Everyone knows that twins can share a special relationship, a very strong bond. Two brothers who we'll call Jack and Ryan Green can testify as to just how mysterious and miraculous that bond can be.

Jack and Ryan were fraternal twins. Unlike identical twins, they were the products of two fertilized eggs and couldn't look more different. Jack was a blue-eyed blonde; Ryan had brown eyes and dark hair.

Ryan and Jack also had distinctly different personalities and developed different interests and skills. But they remained close in many ways. They often expressed identical opinions about events or other people, and each could finish the other's sentences from the time they learned to talk. It was their uncanny ability to sense each other's strong emotions, even when apart, that proved to be the key in saving one's life. Actually, each twin came to the rescue of the other, though those incidents were years apart. The twins and their family still debate the supernatural aspects of the twins' bond.

The first life-and-death situation occurred when the boys were six years old. Ryan had made a friend of a new boy in school named Jonathan. The boy invited Ryan to come to his house to play video games; no adults were home at the time. Unfortunately, Jonathan had not mentioned that they had two cats, and Ryan was highly allergic to cats. A quarter of a mile away in the comfortable suburb of Denver, Jack was receiving the first of a quickening flood of psychic alarms that something was seriously wrong with his twin. Jonathan's cats had triggered a severe allergic reaction in Ryan. He began sneezing uncontrollably. He broke out in hives, especially on his wrists and neck. His face puffed up until his eyes were mere slits. Critically, the tissues of his throat began to swell, slowly but surely choking off air to his lungs. Ryan now was only minutes from death. Panicked, Jonathan called 911 and tried to communicate the urgency of the situation to a dispatcher.

In the meantime, back at the Greens' house, Jack screamed in terror as he literally felt his twin's struggle for breath and subsequent shock. Jack swung into action, grabbing the syringe preloaded with adrenalin that his parents kept for just such an emergency and insisting that his mother drive to Jonathan's house immediately. Ryan got his life-saving shot a full five minutes before the EMT team arrived—five minutes that could have been fatal.

Twelve years passed before Ryan was able to rescue Jack from a life-threatening situation. Again, the mystical bond between the twins provided the paranormal communication vital to saving a life.

It was dusk on a dark Saturday in December, a week before Christmas. Ryan was at home, conscientiously finishing his high school senior thesis. Jack had left early in the afternoon, heading out to ski with some friends; he was uncharacteristically vague about his plans. As daylight faded, Ryan felt a sudden wave of terror and then great pain in his right leg. "Jack's leg is broken," he yelled to his parents. "He's in serious trouble!" But where? Ryan decided to try to mentally contact his twin. As children, they had discovered a capacity for entering the other's mind and "seeing" the past half hour of each other's experience. Jack had been heading for a winter sports site, but which one? Snow was falling throughout the Rockies and visibility couldn't be worse. Trapped in his car by a broken leg, Jack might soon die of exposure and shock if not found promptly.

Concentrating as never before, Ryan began describing Jack's recent actions. "Going through a tunnel on the interstate," he reported. "Must be the Eisenhower Tunnel—taking first exit west of the tunnel—driving along a lake—car skidding on ice, runs into roadside ditch—snow covering the car." Jack's family, studying a map, concluded that he was on Route 6, along the shoreline of the Dillon Reservoir. They gave specific directions to the state police, who promptly located Jack and transported him to a hospital.

Sad Sarah

One of the many ghosts allegedly hanging around the luxurious Brown Palace Hotel is Sad Sarah. She appears now and then on the sixth floor, dressed in a puff-sleeved white shirtwaist and long, dark, tailored skirt, the picture of conservative elegance in 1914, the year of her death. She wears a string of pearls and an impressively large diamond ring. Her pale face is streaked with tears and her slender body is wracked with sobs. Some who've encountered Sad Sarah's forlorn spirit in the halls swear they've heard her mournful crying late at night even when they couldn't see her phantom.

Just who is, or rather was, Sarah, and why is her ghost the picture of sadness? Some local history buffs think they know her tragic story, and a psychic claims to have contacted her in a séance held in a private room at the Brown Palace.

Sarah Hall went from the pinnacle of happiness and optimism to the depths of misery and despair in the time it took to open and read a telegram. That telegram symbolically ended her life. Her dreams smashed beyond hope, Sarah retreated to the luxurious privacy of her elegant suite. Apparently, there she bathed, made up her face, donned fresh clothing, put on her best jewelry and perfume, and hanged herself from a chandelier. The note she left simply said, "I've gone to join Herbert."

A few days before, her fiancé, Herbert Crabtree, had cheerfully boasted that he was the luckiest man in Colorado. He was one of the many who had struck it rich in the gold fields of Cripple Creek. That town and its vicinity were second only to South Africa's famed Witwatersrand in total gold production in the world.

On top of his becoming an overnight millionaire from his gold mine, Herb had received word that his rich Uncle Harry back in England had passed on and bequeathed another fortune to him. Herb needed to go to England immediately to meet with his uncle's executors and make decisions about the sale of the property. Sarah wanted a late-June wedding, so Herb booked a first-class cabin for himself on the first available sailing—a liner leaving Quebec for England on May 29, 1914. Sarah, it was planned, would take a suite at the Brown Palace and await Herb's return while shopping for her wedding gown and looking for a suitable house in which to begin married life.

And so, Herb sailed for England aboard the *Empress of Ireland*, destined for the worst maritime disaster in Canada's history. Herb died on the *Empress of Ireland* along with over a thousand other people. As in the case of the *Titanic*, which had sunk two years earlier, the *Empress* disaster killed more than two-thirds of those aboard.

Sailing down the St. Lawrence River in dense fog, the *Empress* was rammed at a right angle by a Norwegian coal carrier, the *Storstad*. The *Storstad*'s bow sliced open the decks of the *Empress* and cold water rushed in. Many of the portholes on the *Empress* had been left open, because some passengers felt that their cabins were stuffy and overheated. Open portholes allowed more water to enter the *Empress* as she slowly rolled over on her side. The liner sank in only fourteen minutes; only four lifeboats had been launched.

Back at the Brown Palace, Sarah learned that her world had been shattered. Her great love had drowned and her future evaporated like morning fog. It's no wonder that her sad ghost still haunts the Brown palace, weeping and sobbing uncontrollably.

Ghosts of Riverdale Road

Riverdale Road stands out on a highway map because it doesn't follow the rectangular grid so typical of the plains. Instead, it takes a meandering route, arcing northeastward from northwest Denver and following the South Platte River. The river, of course, is the reason for Riverdale Road's irregular course. The forerunner of Riverdale Road was the pioneers' Cherokee Trail. This was also known as the Trapper Trail, because early fur trappers and traders used it. The trail, in turn, was following an ancient American Indian route, which had been used for at least 1,500 years before the first Europeans came to the region.

The current travelers of Riverdale Road—commuters, shoppers, tourists, truckers—cruise along within a spiritual cavalcade of ghosts from the past. While most of the living have no awareness of the many phantoms present along their way, some through the years have sensed or observed spirits moving along or hovering over the road.

Among the oldest ghosts still traveling Riverdale Road are a band of Indian hunters. They are on foot, which means that these spirits date back to a time before the Spanish first brought horses to America. These hunters are weary and weak from hunger. The herds of buffalo they seek have moved to distant grasslands. The hunters are frustrated and desperate. Their whole culture—and the lives of every member of their tribe—depends upon the buffalo. Killing a buffalo provides a quarter ton of excellent meat, as well as hide for making teepees and clothing, and sinew and bones for many uses. When many buffalo are killed, the Indians prosper and live. When few buffalo are killed, many Indians die. The forlorn ghosts of the unsuccessful hunters are looking death in the face. These spirits are particularly sad—not only will they soon die of starvation and voyage to the next world, but many of their tribe will join them.

Other prominent ghosts along the old trail include a pioneer family in a covered wagon. As reported by many witnesses over the years, the wagon is drawn up at the side of the dusty trail. The man and wife have dug a shallow grave, only three feet long. They have just buried a child, dead of typhoid, a disease borne by bad water along the trail. The couple is erecting a crude cross made of cotton-wood. They are in a hurry, as they must cross the Rockies before the winter storms close the passes. Their sorrow is heartfelt, but they cannot linger. Their spirits repeatedly reenact the tragedy of losing a child—one of the worst traumas to haunt parents.

Also seen along Riverdale Road is the shade of a young girl killed in a car crash. She wears a pink satin, lace-trimmed dress of the style favored by senior prom attendees of her time. Her elaborate dress and corsage of red rosebuds sprinkled with silver dust are saturated with her blood. Her bright future, shining with hope and confidence, was shattered by the combination of a tight bend in the road and a boyfriend driving recklessly after downing a whole six-pack. He survived the horrendous accident. Her ghost's face is frozen in a look of disbelieving horror as death approaches at sixty miles an hour.

Beware Riverdale Road in the early morning hours, especially on moonless nights. Death has often traveled this road, and rides it still.

The Professor's Phantom

The professor's phantom hasn't been seen as frequently in recent years as it once was, but if you encounter it, you'll remember. He stands out in a crowd, dressed as he is in mid-nineteenth-century finery: a black frock coat, yellow kid gloves, and a silk top hat. He is a polite young man on a mission to educate the young and pry money from donors to finance his school. If you meet him, it will be in a bar in downtown Denver, because saloons of the better type were his favorite haunts for fundraising.

Oliver James Goldrick arrived in Denver in 1859. His pockets contained a B.A. from the University of Dublin, an M.A. from Columbia University, and fifty cents. His heart contained a passion for teaching and a determination to found a school. He would not charge tuition but would raise money from donations. That's where bars came in.

The "perfesser" as he was called at the time, knew that saloons were the preferred venue for fundraising. Goldrick, it was said, could charm money from men's pockets just by talking with them. He could converse knowledgably and entertainingly on any subject and his behavior in saloons was impeccable. He knew to tip the bartender, refrain from conversation during performances by bare-legged dancing girls, and avoid crowding a serious poker game—"serious" being defined as one in which guns were laid on the table as subtle reminders that cheating was frowned upon.

The perfesser avoided discussing domestic politics after George Washington, instead preferring to regale his listeners with his knowledge of world history, winding up with a discussion of the sexual preferences of European monarchs—always a crowd-pleaser. Then he would pass his hat for donations to his new school, which happened to be the only school in the area. A well-timed round of drinks brought by Goldrick always helped his cause. "The good stuff!" he would admonish the bartender, "make sure it's been aged for several entire days."

With $250 in donations, a tidy sum in those days, Goldrick opened his Union School in a dirt-floored log cabin on Blake Street. He recorded thirteen pupils on the first day: "two Indians, two Mexicans and the rest White." On later fundraising tours, he would bring along a bright student who would impress the crowd by standing on a table and reciting a list of US presidents or reeling off the arithmetic table up to twelve times twelve.

Goldrick's ghost, it is said, still makes the rounds of downtown bars late at night, telling interesting stories and always passing a high silk hat for donations in support of education. Give generously—you do support education, don't you?

Psychic Roommate

Diane Glynn knew, just knew, that it couldn't be true. And yet, it couldn't be just coincidence either. In the privacy and loneliness of her small apartment, she mentally reviewed the events of the past few weeks. Her intellect told her that Rhett could not possibly be clairvoyant or psychic; facts were facts—although Rhett *had* communicated alarm and concern, bordering on panic, minutes before the arrival of very bad news. And that had happened three times now. It had gotten so that Diane almost was afraid to look at Rhett.

Diane had moved to Denver only two months earlier. A recent college grad, she had gotten an attractive job offer from one of the largest banks in the region, a position with almost limitless promotion opportunities for a bright, hardworking economic analyst. She missed family and old friends, so she acquired a roommate. Rhett was, in his way, the perfect roommate. He was very handsome, always eager to greet her when she returned home, and quiet. In fact, their conversations were strictly one-sided, Rhett being a fish.

It would have been nice, of course, for Diane to share her apartment with something warm and furry, but a combination of allergies and lease restrictions ruled out cats and dogs. She had an irrational fear of birds and reptiles never had any appeal to her, so it would have to be a fish. It was love at first sight when she saw Rhett in the pet store. Rhett (named after Clark Gable's character in *Gone with the Wind*) was a betta, or Siamese fighting fish. Diane thought that he was gorgeous, with purple, turquoise, and metallic green all on one little body with long, flowing fins. Diane was assured that bettas were perfectly content in a small aquarium and preferred solitude. "They're highly territorial, very aggressive, and don't play well with others," said the store clerk.

Rhett quickly adjusted to his new home and Diane checked out betta lore online. She learned that they are considered to be intelligent and curious ("How smart can a fish be?" she wondered). She read that bettas like the security of small spaces when resting, so she bought Rhett a ceramic castle that he would hide in at night. Bettas show a combination of fear, aggression, and alarm by flaring their gills, twisting their bodies, and raising their fins when extremely agitated, she read. Horizontal bars of color may appear on their flanks, and they can swim in quick, darting movements, abruptly changing directions.

Rhett displayed an odd amount of curiosity. He seemed to watch Diane as much as she watched him. She got in the habit of leaving the light on in the aquarium cover as a kind of night-light.

One night, as Diane was preparing for bed, Rhett began acting as though his world was about to end. He was in full panic mode, almost butting his head against the glass as he focused on her. What was going on? Finally, he retreated to his castle. About an hour later Diane's phone rang. It was her older sister with bad news: Her husband had been injured in a car crash about an hour earlier. Weird,

Diane thought. Rhett had gone through his all-out panic routine just about then.

Then it happened again a week later. Diane had just gotten in the door and sat down when Rhett suddenly tensed. His little body went rigid, and then he went into his erratic, jerky swimming. Dark horizontal bars appeared on his sides and his bright colors seemed to fluoresce. After a few minutes, he calmed down and hid in his castle.

About forty minutes later, the phone rang. It was her mother. Diane's father, in the hospital for knee surgery, had suffered a heart attack on the operating table. He was expected to recover.

A month later, on a beautiful Saturday morning, Diane was having a late, leisurely breakfast when Rhett suddenly went into his distress display. This was becoming a pattern—a very scary pattern. Was she living with a psychic fish? She snorted with nervous laughter. No, that was absurd. It couldn't be. She waited for the phone call. It was a long wait before it finally came. It was the mother of her closest friend and former college roommate, Ginny. Ginny had been killed in the crash of her boyfriend's private plane. "When?" asked Diane, already knowing the answer. "Around midmorning," was the reply—exactly when Rhett signaled her that something was wrong.

Desperate, Diane contacted a psychic recommended by a friend. "You'll think I'm losing my mind," she told the psychic, "but I think my pet fish senses when a relative or close friend is in danger." After hearing the whole story, the psychic had some surprising words for Diane. "The fish isn't psychic—you are," she explained. "Fish are known to be highly sensitive to vibrations. Sensitivity to vibrations is a survival instinct, so it would make sense that fish could pick up on psychic vibrations from people physically close to them. Your fish isn't anything more than a kind of microphone picking up subliminal whispers from you and amplifying the message, so to speak. You were raised to be very skeptical about the paranormal, so you've unconsciously suppressed and ignored your psychic sensitivities."

Diane is working on developing her newly recognized abilities and continuing to enjoy watching her handsome, sensitive roommate. She was his psychic roommate, not the other way around.

Shades of the Elephant Corral

When it happens, which isn't all that often anymore, it happens very late at night. The phantoms slowly take shape out of the gloom. The living witness catches some unexpected form at the very edge of his or her vision, and then turns for a better look. Is that a person or just a shadow? Sometimes the vision just slowly fades away; sometimes it becomes more solid and boldly approaches, only to disappear before the person's eyes. These mysterious apparitions take many different forms—a variety of sizes, ages, and occupations. Their only common feature, other than being ghosts of course, is that they wear mid-nineteenth-century clothing. All the men wear gun belts, often sagging under the weight of twin six-guns. Most of these apparitions are mean and tough-looking, the sort of thugs you wouldn't want to meet alive or dead.

These horrific phantoms hang out in a very specific location in downtown Denver. It is the vicinity of Blake Street between 15th and 16th Streets in the area between Union Station and Larimer Square. The spirits may be looking for their former home, the hangout and gambling joint known as the Elephant Corral.

The "corral" part of the structure's name was meant as a joke; it was actually a holding pen for people, as the Elephant Corral was a hotel. By contemporary standards, it was a big hotel, hence the "elephant" reference. The hotel was a crudely built haven for crude people, a notoriously dangerous place that was a kind of one-stop shopping center for all kinds of vice.

The Elephant Corral was built of logs. The floor was dirt, the roof canvas, the interior walls simply cotton sheets hung on ropes. Customers brought their own bedding. New York journalist Horace Greeley, who toured the area in 1859, reported that "every guest is allowed as good a bed as his own blankets will make for him."

Many of the hotel saloon's former population—gunfighters, cheating gamblers, violent drunks, sleazy conmen, and tawdry prostitutes—have apparently returned from the realm of the dead to harass the living. One of the many spirits of the old Elephant Corral said to haunt the area is that of "Smiling Ed," the corral's resident undertaker. So many folks were killed in the hotel that Smiling Ed had a contract to bury them at the hotel's expense. It is said that Smiling Ed had an ornate coffin that was used for every funeral. Each corpse was displayed in this box for the wake, and then dumped out at the cemetery, which was also owned by Ed. The coffin was recycled more than forty times before it was finally buried, occupied by Smiling Ed himself. Ed had made the fatal error of commenting unfavorably on a cowboy's moral character and ancestry. His grinning ghost is dressed all in black.

The most frightening of the Elephant Corral's spirits may be that of "Deadeye Dick," as some old-timers call him. Dick is the shade of a gunfighter who loved to gamble. He also loved to win—in fact, he insisted on it. There is an old story that Deadeye was playing cards with a rich gold miner, who held what he thought was a winning hand. "What can beat four aces?" he asked, ready to gather his winnings. "A Colt .38!" was Dick's answer as he shot the man through the heart.

Deadeye Dick is the ghost you'd least like to meet. His phantom swaggers down the late-night sidewalk, carrying two guns and wearing an evil grin. Most of the living flee the scene promptly. The story is that one recent midnight, a visitor from Pennsylvania courageously faced down old Deadeye. The brave young man refused to be intimidated by the phantom bully. The man stood his ground, and it was the spirit of Deadeye Dick who decided to disappear.

Another memorable ghost from the notorious Elephant Corral is alleged to be that of a prostitute called "Fireplug Annie," so named because she was built like a fireplug or street hydrant—a vertical cylinder with no neck and no waist. It was said that Fireplug Annie was quite aggressive about finding customers. She would boldly approach men in the corral's saloon or out on the street and more or less bully them into an intimate transaction. Reportedly, Fireplug Annie liked to wear very large broad-brimmed hats trimmed with ostrich feathers. Should you by chance see her phantom approaching you late some night in downtown Denver, do what stout-hearted gunfighters of the 1850s would have done—walk quickly in the opposite direction.

The Spirit of Buffalo Bill

Shimmering with a faint phosphorescence, the figure gradually becomes more distinct, more solid in appearance. This perceived solidity is misleading, however, as the image can disappear without warning; it is only a ghost. But what a ghost it is! The tall, handsome figure seems to be the perfect representation of the rugged, fiercely independent westerner. And so it should, because the living man had practically created the public perception of the Wild West. Meet the ghost of William Frederick "Buffalo Bill" Cody.

Buffalo Bill's spirit has occasionally chosen to appear near his grave atop Lookout Mountain, a dozen miles south of Golden. Generally, ghosts are more likely to haunt places important to them in life rather than hang about their graves, but Buffalo Bill's phantom apparition has good reasons for haunting his burial spot. His final resting place, at the very top of 7,375-foot-high Lookout Mountain, provides a magnificent view of an iconic landscape of the Old West: endless rolling high plains and spectacular mountain peaks. There, Bill's spirit can not only revel in the unparalleled vista, but it can also enjoy the crowds of curious visitors and the fans who've stopped to pay tribute to his memory.

William Cody very much enjoyed being at the center of attention. In life, he had consciously shaped a theatrical, exaggerated image of himself and successfully marketed that persona as a symbol of the Old West—a west that was changing rapidly even as his show flourished. The sense that the Wild West of romantic myth was being tamed helped Buffalo Bill sell nostalgia.

William Cody was born in Iowa on February 26, 1846. Orphaned at an early age, he became a Pony Express rider at thirteen, riding alone through hostile Indian territory. General Phil Sheridan later made him the army's Chief of Scouts, and he became a renowned Indian fighter. During the Sioux War of 1876, he challenged Chief Yellow Hand to a duel in front of opposing ranks of soldiers and Indians. He killed the chief and the Indians dispersed. Cody also contracted with the railroads to supply work gangs with meat. A fearless and expert marksman, he shot as many as seventy buffalo a day, thus earning his nickname.

In the early 1880s Buffalo Bill organized his Wild West production, embarking on a show-business career that lasted for a third of

WILLIAM F. CODY
MEDAL OF HONOR
INDIAN SCOUT U.S. CAV.
INDIAN WARS
45 1845 ✝ JAN 10 1917

a century and brought him international fame. Cody put on a spectacular show, hiring authentic cowboys and Indians who dazzled the audiences with expert marksmanship and daring horsemanship. Cody made a fortune with his show, but then lost it in realestate speculation. He died in poverty in Denver on January 10, 1917, almost seventy-one years old.

His ghost is a tall, muscular man with long, flowing hair, a luxuriant mustache, and a pointed, carefully trimmed goatee. He wears a tailored western shirt, blue jeans with leather chaps, and beautifully ornate boots, all topped off with a white ten-gallon hat and a large silver buckle inlaid with gold. Cody knew how to present himself, not that there wasn't a real hero behind his carefully burnished public image. The long hair, for example, dates to way before his show business career. His Indian name, given to him by Pawnee scouts in the Indian Wars of 1867, was Pahaska, meaning "Long Hair." His spirit must enjoy reminiscing about those glory days.

The Unsinkable Ghost

The Molly Brown House is a popular tourist attraction at 1340 Pennsylvania Street in Denver. It is restored beautifully and meticulously to its Victorian splendor. Mrs. Margaret Tobin Brown, better known as "Unsinkable Molly Brown," would feel right at home here, even though she died in 1932. There are those who believe that her spirit is, in fact, right at home still. Her ghost haunts her old house in a manner that reflects her character in life: determined, outgoing, friendly, helpful, memorable, and rather theatrical.

Margaret Tobin had been born to poor Irish immigrants. She said later that she wanted to marry money but instead married for love—and got money. James Joseph "J. J." Brown was a poor but hardworking mining engineer when they wed in Leadville. He soon oversaw the development of a particularly rich vein of ore and became a millionaire. Despite their newfound wealth, his wife never forgot her humble roots and organized soup kitchens for the families of poor miners. She helped found Colorado's first female suffrage group and campaigned for stricter mine safety regulations. She was a very bright woman who spoke French, German, and

Russian. She ran for the U.S. Senate in 1909. During World War I, she worked with war relief efforts in France. The French government awarded her the Legion of Honor for her dedication to helping women and children made homeless by war. In the last years of her life, Molly worked as an actress in New York.

While Molly accomplished much in her life, she owed her fame and her nickname to just one event: the story of the luxury liner *Titanic*, which sank on April 15, 1912. It is generally agreed that the brand-new ship was handled recklessly in dangerous waters and that the abandonment of the ship was disorganized, causing the insufficient lifeboats to be launched with many empty seats. Mrs. Brown assisted people into lifeboats before getting into number six, one of the last to leave. It was she who insisted that the partly empty lifeboat turn back to the sinking ship to try to rescue those now jumping into the water. She persuaded the ship's officer in charge to go back and even took an oar herself. Molly's lifeboat was the only one to return to help the other passengers. She bravely ignored the belief that the suction of the ship's final plunge beneath the waves would pull down nearby lifeboats; her actions made her a heroine who was later celebrated in films and a Broadway musical. Her spirited insistence on going back to attempt rescues made her truly "unsinkable."

Today, the Molly Brown House celebrates the approach of Halloween by hosting dramatic readings of tales of the supernatural by such masters as Edgar Allan Poe. It was at one of these readings that a middle-aged woman had to get up in search of a restroom. As she left the room, a costumed guide appeared to sense her unspoken need and wordlessly pointed her in the right direction. Later, on her way out, the visitor thanked the hostess for a memorable event, especially the helpful guide costumed as Molly herself. "She looked exactly like the large portrait of Molly Brown," she said. "Long dark skirt, while frilly blouse, large necklace, and black hair piled on top of her head—she's a terrific impersonator!" "But we have no such impersonator this evening," was the reply.

On another occasion, a family of tourists was enjoying a presentation on Molly Brown's life when the mother happened to glance at the back of the room. Over her shoulder she saw a figure that looked like that in Molly Brown's portrait, leaning against the wall and looking on with interest. The woman nudged her husband and they both turned for a better view, but the figure had vanished.

Whose Park Is It?

Just whose park is it—ours or theirs? Ghost hunters and psychics have reason to wonder, for hundreds of ghosts have been seen there by thousands of people, or so they say. Welcome to Denver's Cheesman Park. Don't pick the flowers, don't leave any trash on the ground, and try not to disturb the spirits of the dead. They already are annoyed enough and they don't like it one tiny everlasting bit. It doesn't pay to anger them further.

The ghosts of Cheesman Park seem to take many forms. To some, the shades of the dead appear as shimmering, transparent outlines of human figures, with a rippling effect like that of rising waves or air heated over a fire. Visitors unsure of their sightings frequently leave the park wearing a puzzled frown rather than a look of horror. To others, however, the ghosts, and the threats, are more substantial.

Many, but certainly not all, of the apparitions are dressed in the cheap, badly worn, patched, and bedraggled clothing of the very poor, reflecting the first known function of the site: a "boot hill" dating to the 1850s, where criminals, friendless transients, and the homeless were hurriedly tossed into shallow graves without ceremony or even coffins. These lost souls include some individuals who exhibit clear hostility toward the living. These phantoms allegedly make menacing gestures as they approach park visitors, only to disappear instantly before their terrorized quarries. Some ghosts seem only unpleasantly surprised by the intrusion of the living, and merely frown as they retreat to their graves.

The most frightening phantoms are those who are missing various body parts—arms, legs, or sometimes heads. Fortunately for the mental health of the living observers, these tend to be but fleeting images, flashing across one's consciousness like shooting stars. Those spirits ignore park visitors, intently concentrating on their eternal hunt for missing body parts. It is a common theme in ghost lore that the dead cannot rest in peace if their remains are not united.

What started as an unofficial boot hill was eventually transformed into a more respectable haven for the dead known as Prospect Cemetery. The newer wave of burials was of embalmed corpses in fancy coffins. After this upgrade, the people and government of the city began to appreciate the fantastically beautiful views from Mount Prospect. On a clear day, the majestic front range of the Rockies could be seen in all of its glory, from Pikes Peak on the southwest horizon to Mount Evans in the west. What a place for a park! Since the deceased were not voting, the decision was made to evict the dead.

In 1893, it was decreed that intact coffins would be transported to new locations. To keep costs down, bodies not contained in coffins would be transferred to new mini-coffins measuring only one foot by three-and-a-half feet. It was a triumph of low-bid thinking. As one city official commented, "the dead lose weight quickly!" It is estimated that between six thousand and ten thousand bodies—most of them just bones—were disinterred with minimal effort to handle them with dignity and respect. An individual's bones might end up in several different boxes, often along with bits and pieces of other bodies. Thousands of the dead, or at least parts of them, likely remain under the park.

The spirits of the dead are restless. They are angry about being disturbed and their corpses being handled so rudely and disrespectfully. Before it was Cheesman Park, it was their eternal resting place. They were there first—and besides, the view is sublime.

Northern Plains

This region in northeast Colorado is bounded by Wyoming and Nebraska to the north, Nebraska and Kansas to the east, and the front range of the Rockies to the west. The region's southern edge is defined by Interstate 70. Most of this region's population is concentrated along the western edge from Boulder to Fort Collins to Greeley.

The pitiful ghosts of pioneers traveling across the dry plains appear in this section, along with a ghost town of drought victims. A murderer's guilt haunts him, leading to his confession, and you'll learn the folly of trusting rattlesnakes. Bigfoot makes a brief appearance, as do the ghosts of a town that moved several times.

Bigfoot and the Genius

It goes without saying that Bigfoot reports are controversial. Usually, though, those who've had an encounter with Bigfoot are believers, while the skeptics and scoffers are limited to the folks far removed from the actual sighting. Not so in the wave of recent Bigfoot appearances near Colorado Springs. The experience of the Cross family children is typical of these recent encounters.

It had been only recently that Bill, aged eleven, and Jill, aged eight, had been judged mature enough to not need a sitter when mom and dad went out for the evening. After all, they would be protected by their Irish setter, Genius, usually called Gene. Genius got his name the same way that NFL linemen get called "tiny." Genius was a long way from smart. After living with the Crosses for years, he would still wait patiently by the door when he needed to go out—but he'd stand expectantly by the hinge side of the door. A true genius he was not, but he was a loyal, loveable pet who fiercely defended his human family against incursions of squirrels, stray cats, coyotes, and perhaps, a Bigfoot.

It was after dinner on a dark winter evening. With their parents out at a show, Bill and Jill had settled in for an evening of computerized socialization via Facebook. All was calm until Gene suddenly erupted in a flurry of frantic barking. He was at the French doors looking out on the back patio. As Bill and Jill followed Gene's line of vision, they saw a heart-stopping sight. Looking back at them through the glass was a seven-foot-tall creature covered in coarse fur the same color as Gene, who was way beyond ballistic by now. Gene recklessly hurled himself at the glass, his barks turning to deep growls. The Bigfoot, whose eyes reflected in red the interior lights, blinked and turned away, retreating into the backyard. Afraid that the courageous Gene would smash right through the doors in his determination to confront the invader, Bill opened the door, strictly against parental orders. Genius bounded out, never to be seen again.

Had the Cross kids really glimpsed a Bigfoot? Several other encounters in the vicinity were interpreted by the observers as hoaxes; "guys dressed up in gorilla costumes" was a common phrase. It didn't help that the recent Halloween season had seen many gorilla costumes in use, many of high quality and realistic appearance.

The fundamental question is, of course, could Bigfoot be real? There is no way to prove a negative. No one can prove that Bigfoot cannot exist; the absence of positive proof is not enough. There was a time, for example, when the scientific community "knew" that the megamouth shark had become extinct two hundred million year ago. The absence of megamouths from the fossil record was proof—at least until one day in 1987 when a live example showed up in a fisherman's net off Laguna Beach, California.

Similarly, the coelacanth, a primitive fish, was assumed long extinct until one was caught off South Africa in the 1930s. Several more have been caught since. The coelacanth didn't go missing, it just went deeper into the ocean.

The fact that Bigfoot-like creatures appear in many Native American legends has been used to "prove" that Bigfoot is just a legend. But Indian legends also describe bears and mountain lions, which certainly exist. Scientists once also scoffed at African legends of the "men of the forest"—large, powerful, intelligent man-like animals—until, of course, they came face-to-face with gorillas.

So could the Cross kids, along with many others, really have seen a giant, humanlike creature? While there is no hard evidence beyond footprints that Bigfoot is real, there is no reason to say that such a creature could not exist. The most skeptical scientists must admit that the climate and ecology of Colorado do not rule out a Bigfoot-like creature and that such animals would find enough to eat. Are the many people who've seen Bigfoot either deceivers or deceived? But assuming that we are sharing the state and continent with a breeding population of Bigfoot, why don't we see them even more often than we do?

Bigfoot is smart. Many people who have reported seeing Bigfoot, particularly in remote wilderness areas, had the uneasy feeling that they were being watched long before glimpsing Bigfoot. Like other primates in the wild, Bigfoot likely has a natural wariness about people. The experience of anthropologists attempting to study chimpanzees in their natural habitats in Africa is instructive. Even though the scientists knew for certain they were in areas populated by bands of chimps, they saw none at all for weeks. When they finally saw the chimps, it was not because the anthropologists had become better trackers, they surmised. It was because the chimps had surreptitiously observed the intruders for weeks and concluded that these humans were no threats. The chimps then simply stopped bothering to hide or run. It is likely that Bigfoot or Sasquatch similarly is seldom careless about being spotted.

Those who accept the possibility, if not reality, of Bigfoot have some distinguished company. In 1893, future president Theodore Roosevelt published a book, *Wilderness Hunter* in which he recounted one of his guide's encounters with a Bigfoot-like animal. Roosevelt evidently accepted the guide's account as the truth.

As the Cross family members like to observe, it doesn't take a genius to recognize a Bigfoot when they see it. Certainly their dog Genius knew that the creature trespassing in his backyard was a potential threat and responded appropriately, most likely losing his life in defense of his human family.

Dearfield's Dear Departed

As often happens, the ghosts are heard much more frequently than they are seen. When the wind is light, the spirits whisper their regrets, their sad laments. As the wind rises, so do the ghostly voices. Their messages of frustration and disappointment become louder and clearer. It might be possible to ignore the meaning of the desperate, breathy whispers, and most try to do just that, but the spirits are as persistent as the once-living people who watched their community literally dry up and die. Welcome to the lonely spiritual remnants of what once was the small town of Dearfield, about twenty-seven miles east-southeast of Greeley.

Dearfield isn't on the map. Its location is marked now only by a diner, a gas station, and one very lonely house. The town was settled in 1911 as an all–African American community, earning its name when the pioneers observed that the hard work expended in making these fields productive made them very dear indeed. It never was big, with a peak population of about seven hundred. The 1940 census reported twelve residents. Now, none but the dead call it home. It first prospered and then dwindled and died for the same reasons as hundreds of other little farm settlements. Despite the optimism and hard work of hundreds of souls, Dearfield just blew away, destroyed by the unforgiving winds that carried off the fertile skin of the earth itself.

There are a variety of reasons why once-vibrant settlements become ghost towns. They all have to do with earning a living. Most of Colorado's ghost towns were mining towns whose ores were mined out. Some towns boomed briefly as stagecoach or wagon train stops, then died as railroads took over. Railroad towns declined as highways became more important, and highway traffic shifting to interstates doomed other towns. Dearfield was one of a long list of towns that died in the great "Dust Bowl" of the 1930s.

There is an old story about farming on the western plains. As eager would-be wheat farmers headed west out onto the virgin grasslands, a demonstration was held of the latest in steel plows. Crowds gathered to watch. Six horses were harnessed to the plow and a long, straight furrow was plowed, overturning the native grasses and exposing the rich, dark brown soil. A Native American who was watching said, "You've got the wrong side up." General laughter followed. The Indian just didn't understand—or did he? The joke turned out to be on the farmers, and it was a bitter joke indeed.

When the western plains first were plowed in the late nineteenth century, no one fully understood the climate there. There turned out to be very few "average" years in rainfall totals. Some years were much wetter than average, producing large crops for the wheat farmers and encouraging the plowing of yet more grasslands. Other years, sometimes several in a row, were much drier than usual, resulting in disaster for farmers. When drought killed the wheat, the unrelenting winds blew away the soil. They also blew away the hopes and dreams of people throughout the dry plains. The dust bowl had begun and there was really nothing the farmers could do, other than give up.

Dearfield's life was short; its death was agonizing, despite the best efforts of its people. The fault was no one's, and everyone's. An understanding of the climate came after hard experience, and much human tragedy. Now the dearly departed spirits are left to moan and mourn the consequences of a misunderstood, highly variable environment. The ghosts of Dearfield might be trying to tell us something about humanity's place in the natural world.

Julesburg's Many Ghosts

There is an old story regarding a driver lost along Highway 138. Spotting an old cowboy walking along the side of the road, the driver pulled over. "Where can I find Julesburg?" he asked. "Depends on which Julesburg you want," was the reply. "You want the first, second, third or fourth Julesburg?" "I guess the one with gas and food available," said the man, trying to keep the sarcasm out of his voice. "I reckon that would be number four—a mile straight ahead. Don't know much about that one. I'm from the first

Julesburg myself, and things are kind of dead there," said the cowboy, just before he evaporated like morning fog in sunshine.

The modern-day Julesburg, the fourth verion of the town, was built on its current site to minimize the effects of flooding from the South Platte. Each of Julesburg's four lives has depended in some way on the town's location along the South Platte River and the availability of transportation routes, not that the river itself was ever useful for transportation. Like many rivers on the high plains, the South Platte is way too shallow for even the smallest of boats. "A mile wide and an inch deep" was the joking description by early settlers, and that was only a slight exaggeration.

The Pony Express and Overland Stage routes followed the South Platte Trail because it provided water for all and grass for animals. A rough-and-ready assortment of traders, Indian fighters, buffalo hunters, adventurers, and desperadoes regularly rode into the first Julesburg to reprovision, make money, spend money, and generally raise hell. They were especially good at raising hell.

The original Julesburg, and its subsequent incarnations, was named for murdering thief and town founder Jules Beni, who had been appointed station master by the Overland Stage. Beni coordinated freight and passenger traffic and knew when gold and silver shipments were coming through. Those wagon trains or stagecoaches would be attacked by marauding Indian bands that, according to survivors, included white men pretending to be Indians.

It was, and still is, widely believed that Jules Beni was in league with the Indians in raiding the wagon trains and stages. Beni was fired, but there was not enough evidence to arrest him. Beni supposedly buried much of his loot at the Italian's Cave, a local tourist attraction about four miles outside Julesburg. An Italian miner, Uberto Gabello, had dug the cave to obtain building material for his house. Since caves were a rarity on the plains, he called his tunnel a "wondrous cave" and charged a nickel to see it. What was wondrous about it, boasted Gabello, was that people were stupid enough to pay to see a hole in the ground. When Jules hid his treasure in the Italian's Cave, he murdered Gabello to keep the secret. Both Gabello's and Beni's ghosts are said to haunt the cave.

Beni's successor at the Overland Company was Jack Slade, a notorious tough guy. The two quarreled and Jules shot Jack in the stomach with a load of buckshot. Jack recovered and swore that he would cut off Jules's ears and wear them on his watch chain. The story is that Slade tracked down Beni and slowly tortured him to death. Slade's ghost, which still haunts the site of the first Julesburg, is easy to recognize: Just look for the two shrunken, blackened ears hanging from his watch chain. Slade is a mean ghost brimming with anger and hatred. He was hanged by vigilantes, not for the murder of Jules Beni, but for "disturbing the peace." He was a loud and abusive drunk, and folks just got tired of dealing with him.

The first Julesburg was completely destroyed by an Indian raid. The town was rebuilt next to the army post of Fort Sedgwick for protection. This second version later was moved to a new site to accommodate the Union Pacific Railroad's choice of location for a construction camp. This third Julesburg once was called "the wickedest little town east of the Rockies"—and there was a lot of competition for that honor. Railroad workers, a notoriously tough bunch, mingled with thugs, prostitutes, gamblers, and soldiers in a wild mix of bars, brothels, gambling halls, and disreputable boardinghouses. The two most memorable ghosts from the third Julesburg are "Blacksnake" Lachut and Gypsy.

Blacksnake was a teamster famous for his proficiency with a long black leather whip, a vicious temper, a kinky sense of humor, and an awesome vocabulary of profanity. He was the acknowledged master of invective, just as he was an artist with his whip. Once, when a drunk accidentally jostled him in the street, Blacksnake used his whip to rip off most of the man's clothing and lash him unmercifully until the poor man bled to death from his wounds. Just for fun, Blacksnake liked to use his whip to snatch cigars out of men's mouths or to break whiskey bottles on bars. His most popular trick in saloons was to use the whip to slice through the shoulder straps of dancing girls' dresses, causing unplanned stripteases. Finally, this sadistic bully badmouthed and harassed the wrong man, who gunned him down in the street. The legend is that the gunman was rewarded with free drinks in any bar in town.

The other famous ghost is that of a young saloon singer known only as Gypsy. Gypsy was a "good-time girl," a sort of part-time prostitute. She was cursed, she said, with the ability to foretell death. When she told a man that he would soon die, he did, within hours. One evening she tearfully embraced her favorite of the moment and told him that he would survive that night only if he went to church and stayed there until dawn. Her friend laughed, ordered another drink, and went back to his poker game. He died within the hour. People began running away when Gypsy approached, afraid to meet her gaze. Shunned and feared by all, Gypsy became an outcast in town. Finally, one evening, she went into a bar and announced her own death, saying she would never see another sunrise. She didn't. Her forlorn ghost still wanders the site of the third Julesburg. Do not look in her eyes.

Pink Water

There are only a few people left in the Fort Morgan area who still can recall the strange case of the Pink Water Confession. The story was briefly famous in the area, but that was nearly a century ago now. This is the story as pieced together by the sheriff at the time, Jack Timberman. Was the "pink water" supernatural or a product of the murderer's guilty conscience? You decide.

Peter Abramavitch murdered his wife, Marie, when both were in their sixties. Like so many other farmers and ranchers on Colorado's plains, Peter and Marie had arrived in the 1870s with high hopes and, as it turned out, unrealistic expectations. The climate, they'd been told, was like that of Russia's great grasslands and perfect for wheat. They found that eastern Colorado's rainfall was highly unpredictable and frequently much too little for wheat. Less than twenty years after they arrived and on the edge of failure, Peter gave up his dreams of raising wheat and switched to cattle ranching. He went deeply in debt to finance a deep well on his property and soon had a windmill pumping up water that was stored in a huge tank near the house. The tank supplied water to cattle troughs in a fenced corral as well as to the kitchen sink. A reliable water supply may have been a miracle, but it was quite an expensive one.

It has been said that poverty can bring out the best or the worst in people. In Marie's case, the continual struggle to pay their bills and taxes turned her into a perpetually complaining nag. Why couldn't they paint the house? Why couldn't they replace the sagging old mattress? Why couldn't she have a new dress? Why?

One day, Peter was facing a perfect storm of disappointments and problems. The new property tax bill arrived. He shuddered as he read the bottom line. The market price for live cattle had fallen again. The bank was getting nasty about his past-due loan payments. Marie started nagging about new shoes. Peter hit her in her head with the garden spade. He kept on hitting her with all his might.

Peter decided that the best place to dispose of her body was next to the cattle watering trough. The cows' hooves would obscure the signs of freshly turned earth. The coule was childless and had no close friends, so he figured that no one really would miss Marie. He spread the story that she had gone to California to visit her sister. No questions were asked. Thinking it was time to retire, Peter put the ranch up for sale.

As it turned out, the first serious inquiry came from the sheriff, who was in the market for an investment property. Seeing the sheriff at his door nearly caused Peter to swallow his false teeth. When he learned that the sheriff had come as a prospective purchaser, Peter launched into his sales pitch. "I have good water piped right into the house from a new well," he boasted, "with plenty for the cattle too. Can I offer you a glass?" With that, Peter turned on the kitchen faucet and proceeded to fill a large glass. Suddenly, he stared at the glass as though it were a tarantula. "Oh my God!" he screamed, "The water is pink! It's pink with her blood! Marie's blood has leaked down into the water in the well!" Within a few minutes, Peter had blurted out a full confession to the startled sheriff.

"How pink was that water?" asked a deputy back at the jail. "There was nothing wrong with the water," replied the sheriff. "After I put the cuffs on old Peter here, I drank down that glass of water. It was cool, clear and sweet—no hint of any blood at all."

Roman Nose Knows

The tall, powerfully built figure is wearing the full regalia of a Cheyenne war chief. Standing atop a low bluff overlooking the cottonwood-choked streambed, the chief appears to be focused intently on the action taking place below. In profile, the man's face has a hooklike outline with a prominent nose that would have made an ancient Roman Caesar proud. The phantom of the great Chief Roman Nose appears to be profoundly disturbed by what he sees, as well he should be. The ghost is watching a misty vision of a crucial battle in the long struggle between the plains tribes and the white invaders. The ghosts below are reprising the Battle of Beecher Island, a bloody confrontation of 1868 that lasted a full week and that became a watershed moment in the struggle for control of the Great Plains.

The Native Americans of the plains were famed, and feared, for their courage and daring in battle. They were bold in the attack, moving quickly and decisively against the enemy. Fate had changed their lives dramatically when they acquired horses, introduced to the plains by Spanish explorers and conquistadors. Before they had horses, the Indians of the plains had a hard life. Killing buffalo on foot required cunning, perseverance, and stealthy stalking. With horses to ride, the nature of the hunt changed to favor those who were bold, fearless, and skilled horsemen. Access to horses changed the war tactics as well, favoring the fast-moving attackers on horseback. Successful leaders like Roman Nose depended on a kind of "lightning war" strategy, overwhelming their opponents with speed, audacity, and surprise. The plains provided little cover for a defending force; fortune favored a fierce offensive by a superior force—except at Beecher Island. Normally supremely confident in his warriors and in his own leadership qualities, Roman Nose anticipated defeat this time, believing that he had defied the fates and the powers of darkness were against him.

A renowned prophet of his tribe had predicted that Roman Nose would become a great leader, provided that he never eat food that had touched metal. This was a symbolic warning not to forsake his people's traditional ways. The Cheyenne had no metal until the whites traded with them. A few days before the battle that took his life, Roman Nose ate bread that had been cut with an iron knife. As soon as he realized his transgression, Roman Nose asked the tribe's most powerful shaman for a purification ceremony; the shaman agreed, but said that it would take some time—time that Roman Nose did not have.

Fifty soldiers and scouts under Col. George Forsythe and Lt. Fred Beecher were moving along the Arickaree River, looking for a small band of Cheyenne said to be harassing whites. They set up camp along the banks of Black Wolf Creek. Roman Nose's judgment was clouded by his concerns about having offended the gods. He could have shadowed the unaware soldiers and attacked them further along their intended route, but foolishly, the chief agreed with his more reckless lieutenants and moved up Black Wolf Creek. The creek's name was a bad omen: According to Indian legends, the black wolf was an evil spirit whose presence or influence must be avoided at all costs. To initiate an attack along Black Wolf Creek was to enter the lair of a devil.

More than a thousand Cheyenne, Arapaho, and Sioux were under the command of Roman Nose. Unfortunately for the Indians, their most effective tactic of sending wave after wave of swift horsemen against the enemy was frustrated by the army's retreat to a small, low island in the creek. When Roman Nose saw this, he knew that the fates had turned against him. He was being punished for defying the traditions of his people. He was doomed. Roman Nose rode into the stream towards the island and was cut down by rifle fire. His warriors, demoralized by the loss of their leader, settled in to an ineffective, weeklong siege of the island. They had to flee when a large force of soldiers arrived from Fort Wallace, Kansas.

The Battle of Beecher Island proved to be a turning point in the southern Plains Indians' resistance against the whites. The ghost of Roman Nose knows that he is looking at the beginning of the end of his people's independence. The phantom personifies supreme sadness at the end of a way of life.

Dead of Night

Nancy was a little nervous. She didn't believe in ghosts, but the cemetery *was* a little creepy. The fact that it was dusk and the light was fading quickly didn't help. The sun soon would be just a red glow on the western horizon, leaving La Porte in the deep purple shadow of the Rockies.

Nancy was on a research mission. Her recently developed interest in genealogy had led the Michigan native to fly to Salt Lake City to use the world-famous Family History Library. There, she learned that an ancestor had been one of the French-Canadian trappers and fur traders who'd founded La Porte. She'd flown into Denver and rented a car, and was now in Bingham Hill Cemetery looking for a tombstone that might provide more information.

She was in luck. "Jean Le Maire" read the headstone, "1820–1877." Nearby stones provided the names of his spouse and children, all duly noted by Nancy. She was so absorbed in recording all this data that she didn't notice the little cemetery was now lit by glowing orbs of light that seemed to float about the tombstones, sometimes winking on and off with pulsating, greenish light.

Then the really scary stuff began. Nancy was walking back to the car when something grabbed her ankle. She tried to pull free but to no avail. She was trapped in near-total darkness; the orbs had disappeared as though someone had thrown a switch. Terror replaced surprise. Slowly, inexorably, cries and moans seeped into her consciousness. Sound replaced sight as the source of her anxiety. It started with the muted sound of an infant whimpering, sobbing as though its heart were breaking. Was the spirit of a dead child calling out to the parents who'd abandoned it in this cold and lonely grave? Soon, a rising chorus of pitiful cries overwhelmed the infant's sobs. Overhead, the rising west wind carried off a layer of dense clouds, revealing a full moon. It was as though a spotlight had been turned on. Now, Nancy could actually see the sources of the agonized cries she'd been hearing. Stiff, awkward-looking figures lurched about, their unseeing eyes staring at the moon. Coyotes howled in the distance, an almost welcome sound to Nancy, who assumed that the coyotes were at least fellow living creatures. Or were they also supernatural participants in this nightmare of an evening among the dead?

Nancy's last conscious thought as she fell asleep was that no one in the world, or at least the living world, knew where she was. Would she be dragged down into a grave by the spirits all around her, never to be seen again?

She awoke to a sparkling clear day of bright blue skies and cheerful bird songs. She was lying in a shallow, rectangular depression—a grave sunken in a few inches when a rotting coffin had collapsed in upon itself. Looking down at her ankle, Nancy saw that what had felt like a skeletal hand clutching at her the previous night was actually a twisted tree root. Had it all been a vivid nightmare, a terrible dream born of exhaustion and a little jet lag?

Nancy still does family history research, but only in libraries and on the Internet. No more cemeteries in the dead of night.

The Guardian's Ghost

Although it happened decades ago, the memory of the incident is still fresh for Mary Lou. After all, it was her life that was saved. The straight facts of the story, minus the ghost of course, warranted only a few paragraphs on page five of the local paper. If Mary Lou had gone public with the whole story, either it wouldn't have seen print at all, or she would have become the subject of a brief flurry of mostly unwelcome attention. Like many who've had an encounter with a ghost, Mary Lou chose to avoid notoriety by keeping quiet about her experience. Only a few trusted friends, sworn to secrecy, were told about it. Mary Lou dreaded that foggy mixture of awe, disbelief, sympathy, and scorn that seems to hover over those brave enough, or foolish enough, to describe seeing a ghost, even a ghost that had saved her life.

That night was Mary Lou's first and only paranormal experience. It motivated her to do some serious research on ghosts. There is, she discovered, a whole subcategory of ghosts called "guardian ghosts." These are spirits of those once-living people—very often members of the military, police officers, firefighters, nurses, or teachers—who had devoted themselves to the defense, protection, or care of others. For these spirits, death does not end their commitment to save, protect, or nurture. Spiritually, they still are on duty. Mary Lou had to smile at the category's designation, "guardian ghosts." Her helpful ghost was that of her deceased legal—and very devoted—guardian, her beloved Uncle Charles.

Mary Lou had been orphaned at age ten. A drunk driver had killed both of her parents, leaving a terrified but unscathed little girl crying in the backseat. Her Uncle Charles was listed as her guardian in case of just such a tragedy. A childless, lifelong bachelor, Uncle Charles proved to be a wise, devoted, and very protective guardian. As Mary Lou reached her mid-teens, Uncle Charles got the news that he had inoperable cancer. "I'll try real hard to last past your eighteenth birthday," he promised Mary Lou. "You shouldn't have to get used to another guardian. I'll always be with you in spirit." He kept his promise and, at eighteen, Mary Lou was on her own, with a small fortune bequeathed her by Uncle Charles.

It often occurred to Mary Lou that Uncle Charles was still her guardian, in a spiritual sense, even though his ashes filled a brass urn on Mary Lou's fireplace mantel. Before making any decision, Mary Lou would ponder what Uncle Charles would have said or done. He had moved on to the role of posthumous guardian and adviser.

On the night that Uncle Charles's ghost saved her life, Mary Lou was driving from Boulder Falls back to Boulder, where she was a student at the University of Colorado. A light snow had fallen and clouds blocked the light from the moon and stars. She was approaching a tight bend in the road when the ghost appeared suddenly in the middle of the road. He was wearing a white shirt that reflected her headlights like a brilliant searchlight. Mary Lou was dazzled by the light and amazed by the apparition. Uncle Charles's ghost held out both hands, palms outward, as though beseeching her to stop. His face radiated an expression of alarm.

Just as her uncle had taught her, Mary Lou took her foot off the gas and lightly pumped the brakes to prevent or minimize a skid. As her car came to a stop at the beginning of the sharp turn, Mary Lou was horrified to see a large tanker truck that had jackknifed on the slippery road. The truck had bounced off the guardrail and demolished it before falling over on its side and spilling some sort of liquid that already was congealing on the road surface. Without Uncle Charles's ghostly warning, she would have found herself on a frictionless surface headed over the edge of a steep drop across a missing guardrail. Her guardian uncle was truly a guardian ghost.

Trail of Death

The trail is haunted, that's for sure. Over the years, hundreds if not thousands of people have glimpsed the tortured spirits of those who died along the Smoky Hill Trail. This cavalcade of ghosts appears on occasion, mostly at night, at the sites of their deaths or the locations along the trail where they first realized the hopelessness of their situations. They were doomed, and they knew it. The Smoky Hill Trail became better known as the "Starvation Trail" and the "Trail of Death."

Before railroads were built, the popular image of America's great western migration was that of covered wagons and stagecoaches. Both traveled the Trail of Death in great numbers. The covered wagons commonly transported whole families heading for homesteads in the west. Stagecoaches were for the wealthy; the standard fare to travel from Kansas City to Denver ranged from $75 to $100, an enormous sum at the time.

None of the pioneer trails were easy. Distances were vast for horses or oxen, and even worse for solitary men on foot. Endless grasslands, steep mountains, and marauding Indians all presented formidable challenges. The Smoky Hill Trail had one advantage: It was a more direct route to Denver from Kansas City than its major alternative, the Overland Trail. The Overland Trail followed the South Platte River, which arches north-northeast up through Nebraska to join the North Platte and eventually flow into the Missouri River; the Smoky Hill route followed the river of that name through central Kansas, and then picked up the Big Sandy River in eastern Colorado. Unfortunately for travelers, the Big Sandy was more sand than water. Unlike the much larger South Platte, the Big Sandy did not flow all year long. By summer, it was dry. The lack of a reliable water supply along the Colorado portion of the Smoky Hill Trail was what made it the Trail of Death.

Many who traveled the Smoky Hill Trail were not families seeking new farms, but single men lured by the gold of the Rocky Mountains. Mostly, they were poor, eager, and incautious about the dangers and hardships of the trail. The far-off glitter of gold blinded them to the realities of crossing the high, dry plains. The lucky ones traveled on horseback; many walked, some pushing wheelbarrows. Scores, possibly hundreds, never made it. They died of thirst, starvation, and exposure. They were killed by outlaws or Indians. If they were buried, it was in shallow, unmarked graves at the side of the trail. Their pathetic ghosts still haunt the dry dusty route that led so many to agonizing deaths rather than to the gold of the Rockies.

Frightening encounters along the old trail are numerous and macabre. A common paranormal sight along the section from Limon to Denver in the late nineteenth century was of a stagecoach filled with skeletons, many still wearing the tattered remnants of clothing. The skeletons of four horses are still in harness. Some travelers, both past and present, swear that they've seen the phantom of a lone rider on a slow-moving horse. As their vehicle draws up alongside the apparition, the image becomes misty and evaporates. Still others claim to have encountered spectral wagons lumbering along the side of the road. The dead men's tragic faces convey their utter despair as the wagon lurches on to their ultimate fate.

You Can't Trust Rattlesnakes

A few old-timers in the vicinity of Greeley might remember the tale of Arthur Field and his trained snake. Even at the time, which was the early 1900s, it wasn't clear whether Arthur had trained the snake or whether the snake had trained Arthur. Anyhow, their relationship ended in disaster—a powerful warning against trying to manipulate nature.

Arthur had an unusual and potentially dangerous hobby—he dabbled in witchcraft. His late mother had always claimed to be the descendent of witches. Arthur had inherited his mother's interests and her book of spells. One magical spell that interested Arthur concerned bewitching animals to do one's bidding. It was customarily used on cats, dogs, owls, and wolves. Arthur Field decided to use the spell on a prairie rattlesnake. Prairie rattlers are a smaller, less aggressive cousin of the fearsome Western Diamondback. The prairie rattler's prey includes mice, insects, birds, and rats, which means it is a friend of farmers, at least as long as it doesn't come in close contact with people.

Arthur was becoming paranoid about his neighbors. In his diseased mind, they were plotting against him. If he could use satanic powers to enter the mind of a snake and control it, he would have a lethal weapon against all enemies, real or imagined.

The book of spells prescribed a rather complicated procedure. It required capturing a young creature, one whose brain was not fully mature. To ensnare the future servant of evil, a noose had to be made from horsehair taken from the mane of a stallion at midnight. The captive animal had to then be kept in a cage for thirteen nights while it was fed a diet of coagulated blood. Every night at midnight, the creature had to be placed within a magical circle of red candles and taught to worship the Prince of Darkness.

Following the directions precisely, Arthur produced a stealthy assassin, with its rattles removed to avoid warning its targets. He named the snake Lucifer in honor of its godfather, if that title could be used. Lucifer's first assignment was killing the wealthy banker who held the mortgage on Arthur's farm.

"I'll need to meet you privately in your bank office after business hours," Arthur told the banker. "I need to renegotiate the mortgage and I'm willing to pay higher interest." At that meeting, the banker was introduced to Lucifer, who made his first human kill. Taking the mortgage from the banker's dead hand, Arthur burned the document and tucked Lucifer back into his coat.

The next victim was Arthur's neighbor, with whom he had been feuding with over water rights. Arthur dropped Lucifer through the neighbor's open bedroom window one night. Lucifer knew what to do.

Together, Arthur and Lucifer created a reign of terror in the neighborhood, at least until one Halloween night. Late that night, Lucifer crept into Arthur's bed and sank his deadly fangs into the man. Awakened and terrified, Arthur screamed "Why?" "Because you neglected to read the last chapter of your mother's book of spells," hissed Lucifer. "On Halloween, all evil spells are reversed. The master becomes the slave and the slave is master."

Always read the whole book. You can't trust the devil and you surely can't trust rattlesnakes.

Rocky Mountains

THE ROCKY MOUNTAINS ARE THE PROUD EMBLEM OF COLORADO, AS EVI-
denced by the jagged skyline on the state's license plates. The Rockies form the north-south backbone of the Centennial State. Gold
mines still dot this large region, which has produced the valuable
mineral for a century and a half. Most of Colorado's considerable
income from tourism is earned here, thanks to Rocky Mountain
National Park, many restored historic mining towns, and the state's
internationally famous ski resorts. Important towns include Estes
Park, Cañon City, Steamboat Springs, Vail, and Leadville.

Here you'll meet the ghosts of a famous early movie star, a gold
miner both fabulously lucky and tragically unlucky, prisoners, and
railroad builders. UFOs appear in two stories, and there is a visit to
the country's most famous haunted hotel.

A Ghost Guards Confederate Gold

Believe it or not, there is a Confederate ghost haunting Poncha Pass
near the tiny town of Poncha Springs. How he ended up in Colorado
during the Civil War is an unlikely but true story. At the time of the
Civil War, Colorado was a territory. The territorial governor was an
enthusiastic supporter of the Union cause, and helped raise eleven
companies of soldiers to fight under the Union flag. Individual en-

listments, however, were split more evenly between the Union and Confederate armies.

Wars are expensive, and both sides wanted to use Colorado gold to finance the conflict. No major Civil War battles took place in Colorado, but a minor skirmish was fought at Poncha Pass. A group of Confederate soldiers had been sent into Colorado with orders to hijack a shipment of bullion from the gold fields of the Rockies. They succeeded in stealing a whole wagonload of gold and headed south toward New Mexico, where they planned to turn east towards Texas. Chased by a posse of lawmen and irate miners, they had almost cleared 9,010-foot-high Poncha Pass when they ran into a Union patrol from Fort Garland. Three rebels were killed but two of the men in gray, badly wounded, managed to escape with the entire crate of gold. The story is that they disappeared into the woods along Pemlican Creek, staggering along with their heavy burden. The Union soldiers pursued the Confederates into the woods but could not find them. The three Confederates who had been killed were buried in a cemetery in Poncha Springs. It is claimed that, for many years afterward, faint bugle notes and drumbeats could be heard near their graves.

No one knows what happened to the two missing Confederates. Did they die of their wounds? Did they succeed in escaping with or without the gold? Are their ghosts still guarding the gold destined for the Confederate treasury? Local legend favors this last possibility.

Many people since have gone looking for the missing crate of gold. For decades after the event, local folks believed that showing respect for the South's cause would increase one's chances of finding the gold. This display of sympathy with the Confederacy was alleged to begin with a visit to the graves of the three dead soldiers. The deceased were to be saluted by standing at attention over their graves and softly humming "Dixie," the unofficial anthem of the South. Then, toasts should be offered to the Confederate States and to President Jefferson Davis and Gen. Robert E. Lee. A glass of whiskey should be poured out onto each grave. Supposedly, the spirits of the dead soldiers would then guide you to the gold. All of this should take place between a half hour before and a half hour after midnight.

Adult leaders and Boy Scouts at a nearby scout camp claim to have seen an older man in a tattered gray uniform wandering through the woods along Pemlican Creek. If challenged, the figure dissolves into mist. On other occasions, the man in the old gray uniform begs hikers for help, but as they go towards him, he disappears.

Two tourists from Alabama recently had an interesting experience as they drove across Poncha Pass on Route 285. They saw an elderly figure trudging along the side of the road. He was wearing a faded and worn Confederate uniform. As their car drew abreast of him, he snapped to attention and smartly saluted them. "What was all that about?" they wondered. Then they remembered the Confederate flag sticker prominently displayed on the car's front bumper. Too bad they didn't stop and ask where to find the gold. The ghost just might have told them.

Alma's Famous Ghosts

The tiny community of Alma, about eighteen miles south of Breckenridge, boasts an impressive set of ghosts. Like most mountain towns, Alma started life as a mining camp, grew stupendously in the gold booms of the 1850s, and then dwindled to a handful of hardy inhabitants as the gold was mined out. The most famous trio of the many ghosts present consists of a dance-hall girl with a heart of gold, a lucky miner who became an unlucky businessman, and a tireless and devoted frontier preacher.

The woman is dressed elegantly in Victorian-era finery. Her long silk dress is black, as is her broad-brimmed hat. A heavy veil preserves the privacy of her grief as she, or rather her phantom, moves about the long-abandoned graveyard. The original wooden grave markers are long rotted away, but the mysterious mourner obviously is familiar with the geography of the burial yard. She moves slowly from one unmarked grave to another, stopping to offer a prayer and place a single red rose on each grave. Focused on her grief, she seems oblivious to the living, but will quickly disappear if approached. She is the ghost of Silverheels.

No one remembers her given name. She was a radiantly beautiful and accomplished dancer who arrived in Alma at the height of its prosperity. She quickly became a favorite entertainer. As was the custom in the early gold camps, fans showed their appreciation for her talents by tossing "pokes"—small leather bags of gold dust—onto the stage at her feet. One admirer fashioned a pair of solid silver heels for her dance slippers. They became her trademark and the source of her nickname, Silverheels.

Silverheels was believed to have accumulated a small fortune, carefully saving all the gold thrown at her feet. Then disaster struck. The town was ravaged by a smallpox epidemic. Hundreds died. Those who could flee town did so. Women were encouraged to move to the comparative safety of Fairplay, six miles to the south. Silverheels, however, chose to stay in Alma. She transformed herself from an exuberant dancer to a devoted nurse. She took care of the sick and comforted the dying. Many men died of the highly contagious and usually fatal disease while cradled in her arms. Perhaps inevitably, Silverheels caught smallpox. She survived, but her lovely face became disfigured by pockmarks. When the epidemic had finally run its course, the "Angel of Mercy of Alma" left town, but returned often to offer prayers at the graves of disease victims. The grateful citizens named a nearby 13,825-foot-high peak Mount Silverheels in her honor. Silverheels' spirit still makes her sad pilgrimages to visit those who died of smallpox almost a century and a half ago.

Another ghost wanders the vicinity of Alma. This apparition is of a middle-aged man dressed in what once was an expensive custom-made suit, now threadbare and faded. His formerly elegant silk tie is now dirty and wrinkled. His handmade English shoes are scuffed and dusty. The misty image of his face is fixed in an expression of bewildered disappointment; he seems resigned to his tragic fate. This is the phantom of Joseph Higginsbottom, better known as "Buckskin Joe."

Buckskin Joe had unbelievable luck, both good and bad. He discovered gold in an unusually rich vein, right on the surface, only a mile from Alma. He went from dirt poor to fabulously wealthy. Joe decided to invest in real estate and business in the then-thriving town of Alma. He soon owned three dance halls, a theater, and five saloons. Life was good. Then the gold was worked out and most people left. Joe's businesses all failed, and he was back in poverty. It is said that he lost his mind along with his money, and began wandering the streets in search of customers for his enterprises. His spirit walks about, still looking for miners out for a good time.

The third famous ghost of Alma is that of "Father" Dyer, an itinerant preacher who had decided to bring the word of God to the raucous, hard-drinking gold camps like Alma in the 1850s. He had been a miner himself, and had led, he said, a life of sin until he "saw the light." He took a job delivering mail so that he could deliver "the good news" along with the mail. You'll know his ghost if you see it—he has a mail sack over his shoulder and a large Bible in his hand.

Beware the Dunes of Death

The human skull looked as though it had been polished, which in a way, it had been. The extremely fine sand from which it protruded had formed a mildly abrasive matrix that, propelled by the near-constant winds, had smoothed the bone to a gleaming finish. When the ever-shifting sands partially uncovered the skull, a relic of unknown age, they contributed yet another puzzle to the mystery of the great dunes.

The origin of the dunes is not especially controversial; it is the dunes' evil reputation as a region of death and disappearance. Legends tell of lost Indians, vanished sheepherders, and even entire wagon trains gone missing among the high dunes. The sands are, in some places, 1,500 feet deep down to bedrock. The dunes commonly reach heights of 750 feet, as tall as an eighty-story skyscraper. These towering, ever-shifting sands form a barren, threatening wilderness from which many have never returned.

Geologists believe that the fine particles of white, red, pink, green, and gray sand are the remnants of the bed of an ancient inland sea. The sea dried up and the prevailing winds blew the exposed sands across the San Luis Valley up against the western flanks of the Sangre de Cristo Mountains. These mountains are so high (Sierra Blanca Peak reaches 14,345 feet) that the sand is trapped, unable to cross over the mountain range.

The eighty-square-mile Great Sand Dunes National Monument was designated in 1932 by President Herbert Hoover, who had the opinion that the only possible value of the "sea of sand" was in its unique, rather forbidding scenery. The desolate dunes can be a creepy place. It is not unusual for the sands to make weird moaning sounds, especially during strong winds or when tourists attempt to slide down the long slopes in an activity known as "sand skiing." At night, especially on moonlit nights, the dunes are particularly eerie and the many legends told about them become even more believable.

Visitors are warned never to venture far into the dunes, as the landscape constantly changes. Dunes grow, shrink, or move, removing landmarks in minutes. The local Indians told tales of web-footed wild horses that appeared along the sand ridges at dusk or dawn. Their webbed feet enabled them to race across the sands, luring Indians to follow them. Anyone foolish enough to venture after them never was seen again.

Early in the period of white settlement, it is said that a pair of sheepherders decided to move their flock from the San Luis Valley to summer grazing lands high up in the Sangre de Cristos. They would need to skirt the great dunes at Mosca Pass. According to legend, the two herdsmen led a pack train of mules loaded with supplies and a herd of one thousand sheep along the flanks of the great dunes. No creature survived the trek.

On another occasion, a long wagon train stopped at the edge of the dunes where a shallow stream of cool, clear water offered an obvious place for an overnight campsite. By morning, the wagons, draft animals, wagonmaster, and all men had vanished, together with all traces of the stream. Was it quicksand, a sudden sandstorm, or something supernatural that swallowed the entire wagon train?

And then there is the story of the cursed family of the dunes. Allegedly, the local Indians had warned the Martinez family not to try to homestead in the shadow of the dunes. The dunes harbored evil spirits and could shift hundreds of feet in one stormy night. The family ignored the warnings. One day their young son stumbled into a distant ranch, dazed and unable to speak. The sheriff found his parents sitting at the table in their little house—dead, their mouths filled with sand and dinner plates heaped with sand. The rancher took the mute survivor into his home and the boy made himself useful tending sheep. One day a sandstorm enveloped the boy; he and the sheep disappeared, never to be seen again.

Be extra cautious amongst the great dunes. They've killed before and will again.

Good Squeezins

Ute Pass has long had an evil reputation. The 9,165-foot-high mountain pass lies northwest of Pike's Peak, on the road between Colorado Springs and Leadville. The pass through dark granite is oriented east–west, and even at midday it is dark and gloomy. The Ute Indians were well aware of its strategic value and kept close watch over it. Enemies of the Ute were routinely ambushed in the pass. The mountain-dwelling Ute were more or less permanently at war with the people of the plains—the Comanche, Kiowa, Cheyenne, and Arapahoe. Ute Pass was where those invading Ute territory were met and defeated. The legends grew that supernatural forces were allied with the Ute warriors. Monstrous, bloodthirsty wolf-men were said to ambush invaders, slashing their throats and greedily drinking their blood.

Unexplained violence seemed to lurk in the neighborhood of the pass. In 1866, for example, a neighbor stopped in to visit longtime local resident Mrs. Kearny. The cabin at first seemed to be abandoned. The table was set for three, the food was untouched, and the teapot was still warm. Further investigation revealed the decapitated bodies of Mrs. Kearny and her son hidden in the attic. No motive was ever discovered nor was the murderer ever identified.

In another mysterious incident, a stagecoach entered Ute Pass carrying five passengers, a driver, and an armed guard. Forty thousand dollars in bullion was aboard. The stage and four horses, together with the seven people and, of course, the gold, never emerged from the pass. Absolutely no trace of the stagecoach could be found, despite a lot of energetic searching for the gold.

A few years later, Gen. William Palmer's secretary rode into the pass and did not emerge. His body was found with a bullet through the heart and a woman's glove and silk handkerchief by the body. The case remains unsolved.

All of these brutal deaths supposedly have produced a small army of savage ghosts in the pass. Many drivers have reported wrestling unseen hands for control of their vehicles' steering wheels. Brakes suddenly fail. Wisps of fog take various shapes—marauding Indians, prospectors leading mules, crazed gunmen—that disappear as quickly as they appeared.

The most fearsome phantoms are thought to be those of the "Bloody Espinosas," two brothers who, in 1867, embarked on a murderous crusade to kill all the Anglos in Colorado. They told friends of a transforming dream that both experienced while camping in Ute Pass. They reported that the Virgin Mary had appeared, descending to earth in a golden cloud, to tell them of their mission in life. They must kill any and all Anglos who were invading what once had been part of the Spanish Empire. No exceptions: Women, babies, and children all must die. The Espinosas killed twelve people in Ute Pass and then went on a spree in which they murdered at least twenty and maybe as many as fifty people before the brothers were killed and joined the fearsome ghosts of Ute Pass. You'll know the Espinosas' spirits when you see them. They are always together and one of them is carrying his severed head tucked under his arm.

The story is that one brother was killed in an ambush set up by a posse of armed miners, but the other one escaped. That Espinosa was tracked down and shot by famed frontier scout Tom Tobin. Tom wanted to collect the reward for the capture of the surviving brother, but he was a long way away from any town. His solution was to cut off Espinosa's head and preserve it in a jar of whiskey. The story is that someone tried to steal the head in the jar. Tom Tobin pursued the thief and, in the fistfight that followed, the jar was dropped and cracked. The whiskey slowly leaked out.

Tobin took his trophy to the nearest bar. "I need a couple quarts of whiskey and a new jar," he explained. "Well, you're out of luck," said the bartender. "I can give you a new jar but the supply wagon is late and we're real low on whiskey." The soggy head was placed in a new jar and Tom Tobin ordered a roast beef sandwich and a beer. As he finished his meal, he heard two cowboys commenting enthusiastically about the quality of their drinks. "Well, that was right good!" one exclaimed. "Good squeezins!" "What's squeezins?" asked Tobin. "The bartender is squeezing some mighty tasty whiskey out of that old head!" was the reply. Sure enough, Tobin watched the bartender pick up the preserved head and squeeze another glass of whiskey from the now-contorted head. "Don't worry," said the bartender, "I'll fill the jar free of charge when our whiskey supply arrives. I'm getting top dollar for the stuff I can squeeze out of your trophy here. There's good squeezins!"

Maybe that's why the severed head tucked under one Espinosa's ghostly arm looks so wrinkled and lopsided. It's been squeezed, hard and often. Make sure your next drink is poured from a bottle.

Pursued by a UFO

Mary Jane Anderson didn't mind her commute at all, for several reasons. She was the assistant manager of a plush resort in Vail. Buying a condo in Vail was just not possible, what with the astronomical real estate values in the luxurious resort. In addition, Mary Jane was not that thrilled with the architectural ambience of Vail, a town that was founded in the 1960s after Interstate 70 was routed right past some spectacular natural ski slopes. The prevailing motif was Bavarian-Swiss-Austrian chalet crossed with late-American glitz. To Mary Jane, it was an imitative style; she much preferred the slightly shabby, worn authenticity of Leadville, a town a full century older than Vail. Leadville was affordable and somewhat funky and Mary Jane loved the old mining town.

Her commute home took her a short distance west on I-70, followed by a straight shot south on Route 24, a scenic treat that never disappointed. This particular May evening would prove to be especially memorable. Traffic was light—the ski season was over and the summer tourists hadn't arrived in full flood yet. Mary Jane had worked late, so it was almost fully dark when she turned south at exit 171, too dark to admire the wildflowers in full bloom.

Then she saw it. It looked like a torpedo with narrow fins flaring at the back. An intensely bright white light beamed from the front of the object while a greenish, flame-shaped vapor issued from the rear of the unique craft.

Until that moment, Mary Jane described herself as an openminded skeptic on the subject of UFOs. Friends whose mental stability and judgment were unimpeachable had confided in her that they had seen aircraft of unusual shapes and sizes, traveling at impossible speeds and executing unimaginable maneuvers. They had not gone public about these experiences out of fear of ridicule.

Now Mary Jane was having her own sighting. The UFO began playing a cat-and-mouse game with her. The UFO would hover near her, often just in front of her car and only a few yards above the highway, and then abruptly zoom ahead. After stopping suddenly a few miles ahead, the alien craft would swoop back towards her on a seeming collision course, only veering away at the last possible second. It would then hover over her like a helicopter. During the hovering phases, Mary Jane's car would stop running and anything electrical—the lights, radio, dashboard instruments—would die. A bright light flooded her car, the light so intense that she could see her bones through her skin and flesh. Her watch froze, never to function again. Then the UFO accelerated towards the horizon; the car's engine restarted on its own, and the game repeated.

Finally, when Mary Jane was only a mile away from home, the UFO sped away to the south, flashing its lights as though it was making a playful gesture of farewell. She never saw it, or anything like it, again. She has told only a few close friends about her unnerving encounter.

The Gang from Robbers Roost

Just west of La Porte, State Highway 14 is designated an official scenic route. The family of tourists from Ohio had picked a perfect day to enjoy this gateway into the spectacular Rockies. It was early fall in the canyon of the Cache La Poudre River. The wine-colored rocks varied in hue from deep maroon in shadow to brilliant scarlet in sunlight. The bright yellow leaves of the aspens contrasted with the dark greens of the conifers, all under a magnificently blue sky with high white clouds. It was so glorious that the kids in the backseat spontaneously stopped squabbling. It was a memorable day; it became even more memorable when the ghosts showed up.

At first, of course, the family had no idea that they were seeing ghosts. They were astounded when the spectral trio suddenly darted onto the highway from the cover of a large grove of conifers. They were dressed in classic nineteenth-century cowboy gear: well-worn jeans, cowboy boots, leather chaps, checked blue shirts, black leather vests, and broad-brimmed felt hats. Each ghost had a Colt revolver, all of them pointed at the family. It was such a perfect reproduction of a scene from a classic western movie that the father began looking around for a film crew as he stopped their SUV. Surely someone would yell "Cut!" and the family would be waved on impatiently.

But there was no film crew. In fact, there was nobody else in sight. The family now was quite alone with the three thugs on horseback. No one said anything. The tourists were mute with surprise and terror. Their attackers were menacingly silent, gesturing with their guns that the family should get out of the car. Almost paralyzed with fear, they complied. For what seemed a very long moment, the family stood frozen in position beside their vehicle, hands held tremblingly aloft, wondering if this was their last moment on earth.

Kapow! The explosive sound startled everyone. The family watched in amazement as what seemed like a reddish cannonball came hurtling across the road, crashing into the trees behind the robbers. In a flash, the thugs and their horses were gone. They didn't ride away; they just disappeared as though the earth itself had cracked open and swallowed them.

The parents and children just stood there for a long moment wondering what on earth had happened. Then things got really interesting. A state police cruiser stopped right behind them with all its lights flashing. The trooper got out and approached them. "Any reason why you folks are stopped smack in the middle of the road?" he asked. "Did your engine die? Do you need help?"

The mother decided to act as family spokesman, the others apparently having lost the power of speech. She told their story to the clearly skeptical state trooper. The younger son suddenly spoke up, pointing to a swath of freshly broken tree limbs by the side of the road. "That's where the cannonball hit!" he said. "You can't ignore that." The trooper replied, "Yes, something crashed into those trees, but it wasn't an artillery shell. It was a falling rock. It happens now and then, especially this time of year. Water goes into cracks in the rocks, then freezes during these frosty autumn nights. The crack becomes a split, and eventually the loosened chunk of rock falls down."

"That's not what happened," said an unexpected voice from the backseat of the police car. "You saw some ghosts from Robbers Roost, right up the cliff there. A bunch of robbers used to hole up there and rob travelers on the old La Porte-to-Fort Laramie Trail. That there Robbers Roost was such a natural fort that the army had to use a cannon to persuade the bad guys to give up."

"Pay no attention to old Sam there," interjected the trooper. "I picked him up drunk as a skunk and I'm taking him home. He's harmless but he likes to tell old stories."

So was it just a falling rock or was it a ghostly cannonball that chased off the phantom robbers from Robbers Roost? The tourists are inclined to believe old Sam, even if he is a drunk.

The Ghost Who Ran Out of Luck

Horace Tabor's ghost is unusual, which is not a big surprise considering that the living man was a flamboyant original. Horace's spirit is said to appear in two strongly contrasting moods and in at least three venues.

Tabor was one of the luckiest men alive. He was also one of the unluckiest men alive, for he died a badly frustrated, embittered, and abjectly impoverished man. He had gone from poverty to fantastic riches and back to poverty.

The character that shows up in phantom form at the Tabor home, now a museum, in Leadville is that of a self-confident, boisterous man decked out in a splendid suit with a gold-embroidered waistcoat, a tie held in place with a huge diamond pin, and gold and diamond rings on several fingers of each hand. An even more flamboyant version of this newly rich persona is alleged to haunt the Tabor Opera House in Leadville. His ghost there usually shows up in his private box. Horace had built his opera house more as a boastful gift to his adopted hometown than as a money-making enterprise. At the height of his wealth in the 1890s, he was concentrating more on spending than making money.

The face of the woebegone ghost at Leadville's Matchless Mine Cabin, sometimes known as Baby Doe's Cabin, alternates between horrified disbelief and mournful acceptance of his fate. This version of Horace Tabor's spirit reflects his sudden descent into poverty. Here, it is claimed, his ghost appears as a faint image looking over the shoulder of the clearer form of Baby Doe's ghost—a ghost haunting a ghost.

Horace Tabor was a Vermont stonecutter who decided that the difference between a stonecutter and a gold prospector was location. Vermont quarried marble and granite, while Colorado mined gold. Horace, his first wife Augusta, and their young sons joined the swelling ranks of the "Pikes Peak or bust" crowd of hopefuls. Tabor's claim produced only two thousand dollars worth of gold. Disappointed, he opened a small store in a mining camp called Oro. The area around Oro had yielded modest amounts of gold, but miners had to dig through and dispose of large quantities of heavy black sand to reach it—a major nuisance. Then somebody thought to have the black sand assayed. It was carbonate of lead, containing a lot of lead and a whole lot of silver. Oro, population about two hundred on a good day, was renamed Leadville and gained ten thousand inhabitants.

Storekeeper Tabor grubstaked two German shoemakers, who knew nothing at all about mining, to seventeen dollars worth of groceries and a jug of whiskey in return for a share of their find, if any. The ex-shoemakers drank the whiskey and took a nap under a large pine tree. When they woke up, they decided it was better to dig in shade than in sun, and, by pure luck, hit on the purest vein of silver ore ever found. Tabor made one-and-a-half million dollars from his share, reinvesting his money in the Matchless Mine, which earned him another nine million dollars.

The wealth inspired Horace to enter politics, and he was elected lieutenant governor. He gave Leadville a fully equipped fire department and built his opera house. One night at the opera house, Tabor was intrigued by a voluptuous "Oriental dancer" who showed some leg and wore a low-cut gown. In appreciation for her erotic dance and in hopes of a later, more private performance, Tabor tossed a handful of silver coins onto the stage. A business rival threw her a double handful. Tabor, in turn, tossed more coins and sent an employee to open the vault and bring more money, including gold coins. His rival responded in kind. A literal rain of money fell on the stage. The dancer harvested $5,000 from the stage, and then refused both men's invitations to a late supper.

Tabor's wife was not pleased; Tabor later divorced her and married a lovely young divorcee, Elizabeth "Baby" Doe. Then, disaster struck. The financial panic of 1893 absolutely wiped out Horace Tabor. He died in Denver in 1899, a ruined man. Baby Doe lived until 1935, occupying a crude shack next to the abandoned Matchless Mine—the mine that once had seemed to be a limitless source of riches but now was exhausted and forlorn, just like the ghosts that still haunt the place today.

Ghosts of a Ghost Town

The shiny silver-star badge of an officer of the law is the first thing the observer notices. The second thing they observe is the fact that the star is pinned to a very bloody plaid shirt worn by the tall, mustachioed figure staggering down the dusty road. He is holding a revolver in each trembling hand and looks like he is about to collapse. Suddenly he falls to the ground and then, astonishingly, he disappears in a swirl of dust. He is one of several ghosts who are said to appear with some frequency in the ghost town of Tincup.

Tincup is located on a very rough road northeast of Gunnison. In 1880, it had two ore smelters processing gold and a population of more than 1,200. It also had fifteen saloons mining gold out of prospectors' pockets. Tincup got its name when a prospector used a tin cup to wash gold particles out of stream gravel. It was that easy, at least in the beginning. It also was easy to lose gold to the hosts of thugs, adventurers, swindlers, bartenders, and prostitutes that thronged to the town following news of a gold strike. Like most little mining towns of its day, it was a notoriously wild place. It is said that peace officers had such a short life expectancy that the job's fringe benefits included a free funeral and complimentary burial plot.

One of Tincup's most colorful ghosts is that of a dancehall girl that everyone calls Lil. She apparently likes to appear just before nightfall and is dressed, if that's the right word, in very little: black fishnet stockings, sequined corset, and some strategically placed ostrich feathers. Lil's ghost goes into a dance routine, gyrating to music only she can hear. From a distance, Lil looks youthful and lovely, but as the vision gets closer, she seems to age and her costume appears to deteriorate. The stockings have large rents in them and the feathers are shedding small pieces. Her satin shoes are scuffed and dusty. Her thick layers of stage makeup are cracked and dry, flaking away from her face to reveal a cobweb of fine wrinkles. The sagging pouches under the dancer's eyes are the color of charcoal. Those observers who have not already fled the scene then witness a startling and gruesome transformation. The flesh seems to melt off Lil's bones and skull, leaving a dancing skeleton. The figure dissolves in a shimmer of bright dust.

A much less troubling vision is that of a child about three years old. The little boy, dressed in ragged clothing and not wearing shoes, appears out of nowhere. He is chasing a bright red ball that bounces along in front of him. If he catches it, he fumbles it and then continues the chase. The red ball will be seen to reverse direction in midair as though it were a living thing intent on avoiding capture. An old legend advises the living not to try to get the ball—catching it means catching your own death.

Ghosts of Marble Cave

Nothing about Marble Cave is welcoming. It lies deep in the Sangre de Cristo Mountains, north of the Crestone Needles and west of Westcliffe. The entrance is difficult to spot, even though explorers of nearly a century ago are said to have painted a Maltese cross above the entry tunnel. A bitterly cold air current blasts out of the mouth of the cavern, strong enough to extinguish any lantern's open flame. That same cold wind is said to often make a very human-sounding moan as it rushes out of the bowels of the earth. Are the moans a natural phenomenon, the result of air passing through narrow, twisting tunnels? Or are they supernatural echoes of past horrors and warnings of troubled spirits present deep underground?

Marble Cave may have nothing to do with marble; geologists think that Marble Cave itself is actually a volcanic fissure. The cave wasn't always known by its current name. Old Spanish legends referred to it as *La Caverna del Oro*, or the Cave of Gold. According to legend, the Spanish conquistadores discovered gold there and used Indians as forced labor to mine the material. There is plenty of historical evidence that the Spanish did this elsewhere in their New World empire, so it is possible they did this in the Cave of Gold as well.

Ancient legends also hold that not only did Spanish explorers mine gold in the cave, they also stored the bullion there until it could be safely transported down to Mexico. The story is that, deep inside this cave of gold, stout oak doors braced with wrought iron closed off storage rooms carved from solid rock. Inside those secret rooms lies a vast fortune of gold. According to Indian folklore, that treasure is tainted by innocent blood.

Traditional Indian beliefs held that, while the sky was the domain of the gods and everything good and positive, the underworld was the lair of evil and negative energies. Indians avoided going into caves at all costs, believing that any place out of reach of natural light from the sun, moon, and stars was the abode of evil spirits.

Accordingly, the Indians were terrified when the Spanish forced them to work underground, completely against their traditions. The Indians allegedly attempted to simply not work, producing no gold during their enforced stay in the mines. The Spanish supposedly retaliated by assigning each miner a daily quota of gold. If you couldn't hand over a few ounces of the mineral at the end of the day, you were not allowed to come back to the surface until you did so. Water was provided, but food was not. Some Indians died underground. Their corpses were left where they fell as a gruesome warning to the living workers. It is the spirits of these dead, trapped deep underground for eternity, that haunt the cave, moaning in abject terror at never again seeing natural light. These tragic phantoms are very angry about their fate and allegedly try to smother anyone who invades their tunnels of death. Some legends assert that these ghosts will trip and push the living, attempting to cause fatal falls down the mine shafts.

In 1920, the first organized scientific exploration of Marble Cave in the modern era took place. Crude wooden ladders were found, as were hand-forged iron tools estimated to be at least two centuries old. At least a dozen skeletons were found more than two hundred feet below the surface. A 1929 expedition descended more than five hundred feet below the entrance but had to abandon its attempt to reach the bottom because of dangerously loose rock in the shaft. All of the cave explorers reported being disturbed by the loud moans that seemed to intensify as they descended deeper. Strong air currents repeatedly extinguished lanterns and candles, and flashlights exploded. Several people were seriously injured by falling rocks. All of the adventurers were haunted by terrifying dreams for months afterwards.

Perhaps it is just as well that the cavern has not been developed as a tourist attraction. Disturbing the ghosts of Marble Cave most likely would be a really bad idea.

Host with the Most

The man is the picture of elegance. He is dressed in the height of Victorian fashion: an immaculate, beautifully tailored, dark gray suit; an embroidered silk vest; and a bright tie. The gentleman is evidently prosperous, as a diamond stick pin fastens his tie, a heavy gold watch chain is stretched across his ample stomach, and more diamonds sparkle on his fingers. Often, the figure is holding a wine bottle. Don't wait for him to fill your glass though, for his form is likely to disappear in an instant. You have just met the phantom of Louis Du Pay—restaurateur extraordinaire, master chef, wine expert, architect, decorator with impeccable taste, and insufferable snob.

Louis built and ran one of the most elegant French restaurants in the world. His cuisine was internationally renowned, his wine cellar the envy of connoisseurs everywhere, his reputation spotless. He opened his Hotel de Paris in Georgetown in 1875 and ran it until his death in 1900. It was his pride and joy. Many think that Louis never really left his beloved hotel; his spirit is still there, they say, and he materializes from time to time, whenever it suits him.

The Hotel de Paris survives as a museum. Today, just as in 1875, it is filled with the finest examples of French luxury and art. Gilt seems to drip from the furnishings; it covers mirrors, paintings in elaborate frames, sculptures, wall sconces, door frames—indeed, the whole building. It is claimed that genuine diamond dust adds a special sparkle to the huge mirrors.

After an aimless life of unsuccessful ventures and dead-end careers, Louis Du Pay finally ended up in the right place at the right time. Georgetown's mines produced an estimated hundred million dollars worth of gold, silver, copper, and lead, and miners wanted to spend it elegantly. Uneducated ruffians who used to drink rotgut whiskey and eat beans and flapjacks wanted to sip vintage champagne from crystal flutes and eat exquisite French food from English china. They craved to live like, and be recognized as, real gentlemen. This is where Louis Du Pay came in.

Louis was born in France to wealthy aristocrats. He squandered his inheritance, served in the French and American armies, worked as a journalist in Paris, London, and New York, and prospected for gold in the Rockies. He impressed his fellow miners with his fine manners, sophisticated tastes, cooking skills, and knowledge of wine vintages. He was the ultimate wine snob, and this impressed his fellow miners. Those who became instant millionaires desperately craved the worldly elegance that Louis seemed to personify. When Louis was injured in a mine explosion, his friends decided to finance his dream: a first-class French restaurant for Georgetown.

His Hotel de Paris was an instant success, due in part to Louis's imperious snobbery. He turned away anyone who was not suitably dressed or behaved. Acceptance was proof of one's social standing, like admission to an exclusive club. Louis's arrogance was famous, and contributed to his success. He refused to pay any taxes, saying that he'd rather burn down his establishment. Local government officials, eager to be welcomed into his hotel, let him get away with this.

Louis was the acknowledged social arbiter of Georgetown. His whole establishment was a lesson in architecture, interior design, and fine arts, as well as in fine dining and elegant drinking. He saw himself as an educator of sorts, and indeed, many people actually opened books to prepare for the sophisticated conversations led by their host.

Is that a self-satisfied, superior, rather disdainful smile on the lips of Louis Du Pay's ghost? You'd better believe it. Hope your clothing and deportment meet his high standards. He was the ultimate host with the most, boasting the most elegant restaurant, the finest wine cellar, the best food, and the most interesting conversations this side of Parisian salons. Now he is the most interesting ghost in Georgetown.

The Hunter Becomes the Hunted

The dreams certainly were intriguing. They were somewhat disturbing, but stopped short of being truly horrific. The most interesting facts about the visions were that they were repeated nightly, and that husband and wife experienced almost identical dreams.

The couple, Greg and Susie Potter, was vacationing in Estes Park, a very comfortable resort town set within some of the most spectacular mountain scenery on the continent. The dreams began the first night of their one-week stay there at the gateway to Rocky Mountain National Park.

Their dreams always began with the close-up view of a man running. He is running flat out, as fast as he possibly can. His red, sweaty face is contorted by his strenuous physical effort. His breathing is labored and ragged; he is at the edge of collapse from complete exhaustion. His eyes have an unfocused stare of total terror. It is clear now that the man is quite literally running for his life. In the dream, the view shifts from a close-up of the man's agonized form to include a broader view of his situation. The reason for his evident panic becomes clear. He is being pursued, at least in most dreams, by a thundering herd of buffalo. In a few instances the pursuers are enraged grizzly bears. The dream continues to the same climax—the moment that the running man finally collapses, brought down by his ferocious, frantic, and persistent pursuers.

Oddly, the young couple who experienced these repeating dreams did not share the mysterious man's terror. As the dreams repeated with minor variations, the dreamers began to notice a group of Native Americans in the background who seemed to be watching the action intently. Their faces were impassive, displaying no sympathy for the plight of the running man.

What did all of this mean and why would two people have almost identical dreams? When they returned home, Greg and Susie talked with a psychic, who explained that they had vacationed in an area that was steeped in the emotional energies of some highly traumatic events in the past. The presence of other, emotionally detached observers—the Indians—was significant to the psychic. She believed that the Potters' dreams actually related to the strong perceptions, and perhaps wishes, of the Indians. "Read up on the local history of Estes Park, particularly the history involving Indians, buffalo and bears, and a terrorized white man."

It wasn't long before their readings revealed the story of George Gore, for whom the Gore Mountains were named. Sir Gore, a member of the Irish aristocracy, had led a memorable hunting expedition to Colorado in 1855. He is known to have hunted in the north, middle, and south parks of the Colorado Rockies. These "parks" actually are huge natural meadows occupying high mountain basins. Their lush grasses attract deer, antelope, and buffalo, which in turn attract grizzly bears and mountain lions—creating a hunter's paradise.

Sir Gore was the type of arrogant aristocrat who hunted only for the thrill of killing. He did not hunt for meat or hides, but rather for glory. Quantity counted; he wanted to set new records for the number of animals slaughtered. It is reported that his hunting party included forty servants—cooks, "beaters" to flush game, wagon drivers, skinners, and assorted hangers-on. One hundred and twelve horses and twenty-four oxen transported this enormous, luxuriously outfitted killing machine. Gore and his friends boasted about killing three thousand buffalo and forty grizzlies. They didn't bother to count antelope and deer. The local Native Americans were horrified by this wanton slaughter of the animals upon which their food supply depended. Allegedly, they considered killing Gore and his party, but decided it would not be worth a full-scale war with the whites. Instead, they put a curse upon Sir George so that his spirit would be chased for all eternity by the spirits of the animals he killed. It was this scenario that reached into the subconscious of the Potters.

Gore's spirit's eternal flight from pursuing buffalo and grizzlies is the environment's justice. The hunter became the hunted, for all eternity.

The Most Famous Haunted Hotel

The landmark, Georgian-style hotel opened in 1909 and is thus in its second century of graciously hosting the rich and famous—as well as the ghosts, for there is widespread agreement that the Stanley Hotel is haunted. Among the long list of prominent people who've stayed at the Stanley is author Stephen King, the acknowledged master of horror. The Stanley Hotel is widely believed to have inspired King's classic novel *The Shining*.

The Stanley was built as a luxury resort in a spectacularly beautiful setting, Estes Park. Freelan Stanley and his brother invented the Stanley Steamer, a steam-powered car that was popular in the early 1900s. He decided to invest his automobile profits in Estes Park, preferring to live amidst the area's numerous high peaks. To Freelan and his wife, Flora, this was paradise on earth. They never wanted to leave, and apparently, they never did.

Freelan haunts two of his favorite places in the hotel: the bar and the billiard room. In the bar, his distinguished face hovers over a comfortable chair in a corner, smiling like the gracious host he once was, and sipping from a squat crystal tumbler of scotch and pure Rocky Mountain glacial water. He was fond of saying that Fall

River water, once frozen in glaciers for thousands of years, was so naturally cold and clean that it was the perfect complement to whiskey from the Scottish Highlands. If you are a drinking person, try his favorite drink. A few might help you see Freelan's ghost. His phantom is also believed to hang out in the billiard room where he enjoyed many an evening making new friends and coaching inexperienced players. He liked to lean over new players and gently guide their arms to more professional positions and angles, whispering advice in their ears. If you receive such help from an unseen source, follow the advice.

Flora Stanley's ghost likes to play the piano in the hotel ballroom. She is said to be quite good, although her repertoire doesn't include any music written after about 1929, the year of her death. Flora and Freelan's spirits do not appear together. They got along fine but, in their day and social level, men and women socialized separately after dinner, which is when their ghosts are most likely to appear.

Other, somewhat less famous ghosts are said to haunt the old Stanley. Rooms 217, 401, and 407 are among those in which many guests have reported apparitions or strange, unexplainable events. Glowing, greenish-white orbs are said to float in the air in those rooms, moving about rhythmically if any music is played. Lights may be turned on or off by unseen hands. One elderly couple, guests in room 401, reported an encounter with a ghost who repeatedly turned out the bathroom light, which the couple had left on as a nightlight. The couple decided to calmly explain to their unseen fellow room guest that, at their age, late-night visits to the bathroom were an inconvenient but necessary fact of life. Could the spirit please leave the light on? This appeal evidently impressed the phantom. For the rest of their stay, the light switch was not touched, at least not by the ghost.

Guests whose rooms are near the elevators sometimes complain about the elevators moving noisily up and down the shafts continuously very late at night. Those bold enough to open their room doors and look down the corridor report that people dressed in 1920s-style tuxedoes and evening gowns can be seen entering or leaving the elevators—but the elevator doors remain closed. All of this occurs, supposedly, between two and four in the morning. Loud ragtime music can be heard coming from the ballroom late at night. On investigation, no one is there.

The Stanley surely is one of the few hotels in the world to offer tours of the alleged supernatural geography of the building, with detailed histories of the several ghosts and their favorite haunts. The spirits of the Stanley Hotel seem to be benign for the most part. Unlike in the hotel of King's novel, no really horrific experiences have been recorded, at least not yet. Enjoy your stay.

Prison Ghosts

Cañon City's location is well suited to the tourism business. It lies at the mouth of the Royal Gorge, as the Grand Canyon of the Arkansas River is known. At Cañon City, the Arkansas emerges from its spectacular canyon, over a thousand feet deep, out onto the plains to begin a 1,900-mile open-country run to join the Mississippi. The canyon has been used as a movie set since silent film days and has provided magnificent scenery for films like *Cat Ballou* and the 1969 version of *True Grit*. Just a few miles upstream from Cañon City is a major tourist attraction: Royal Gorge Bridge, the world's highest suspension bridge.

While the scenery brings plenty of visitors, it is the other major prop of Cañon City's economy that has provided its most horrific ghosts. With thirteen correctional institutions, Cañon City is the prison capital of Colorado. There is an old story that, back in 1868, Cañon City was offered the choice of the territorial prison or the territorial university. Supposedly, Cañon City's leaders chose the prison because it was an already-established institution and "seemed likely to be better attended." In a way, Cañon City's two main industries—tourism and the penal system—are related.

For many years, the Colorado State Penitentiary was open to visitors who paid for tours. Tourists could view the cellblocks, workshops, ranches, farms, dairy, and cannery, watching prisoners grow and process much of their own food. Now, tourists can visit the Museum of Colorado Prisons and admire the old gas chamber, along with exhibits of inmates' weapons, "disciplinary paraphernalia," and original prisoner crafts and artwork. Although not an advertised attraction, the ghosts of some celebrated prisoners and guards are alleged to haunt the prison, including the spirits of the infamous cannibal Alfred Packer and twelve-year old murderer Anton Woode.

The most gruesome ghosts are said to be those of both the victims and perpetrators of a deadly prison riot on October 9–10, 1929. Apparently, the trouble began with a spontaneous prisoner protest about the quality of the food and the harsh disciplinary measures. The protest became violent, and six guards were disarmed and held hostage. A convict named Danny Daniels emerged as the leader and threatened to kill the guards unless he and his men were given freedom. The warden refused. Daniels killed the guards one by one and tossed their mutilated bodies out of a high window. He said that he liked to hear the splat when they landed in the courtyard. When the prisoners had killed all of their hostages without achieving their freedom, despair set in. Daniels shot all of his fellow conspirators, and then turned the gun on himself.

The ghosts of the guards are a memorably horrific sight. Their uniforms are drenched in blood. They stumble about, bent nearly double in agony. Daniels had shot them in the gut in order to prolong their terrible pain, and then mutilated their corpses. The ghosts of the prisoners stare vacantly out of dead eyes, blood oozing from the merciful head shots delivered by their leader. Daniels himself is marked by the bullet wound in his right temple, a feature of his suicide.

These prison ghosts are most often seen in the cellblock where the violence took place, but they are said to appear also in the prison cafeteria and even out in the old farm building. October is the best month to see them.

The Shade of the Manassa Mauler

The tiny community of Manassa is home to about one thousand living souls and at least one ghost—and a famous ghost at that. The alleged ghost is said to show up on an unpredictable schedule, usually when a handful of visitors appears at the little museum that occupies his restored boyhood home. The ghost, like the living man, hates to disappoint his fans. He has been described variously as an outgoing, robust teenager; a broadly smiling, immaculately dressed businessman; or a powerfully built man in his late twenties, dressed for the boxing ring in satin shorts, heavy leather boxing mitts, and black shoes. Why is there a range of visual images? Perhaps the spirit of the boxer is unfocused but omnipresent, allowing the living to fill in the details through their own expectations and imaginations.

Meet the spirit of William Harrison "Jack" Dempsey, aka "The Manassa Mauler." The legendary heavyweight champion of the world was born on June 24, 1895; his father was Irish and his mother a mixture of Irish and Cherokee. Jack became a six-foot-one teenager who built his muscles the hard way: by working on the railroad and in the gold mines at Cripple Creek. At Cripple Creek he accepted a challenge to take on a locally famous prizefighter. Dempsey fought a grueling, bloody, bare-knuckle battle and won $50. He decided that boxing paid better than the mines and turned professional. By the time he was twenty-four, he was the world champion, a title he held from 1919 to 1926. Out of eighty-three professional bouts, Jack won sixty-six, fifty-one of them by knockout. He had eleven draws and lost six. Only once was he knocked out.

Unlike all too many other boxers, Jack Dempsey knew when to quit the ring, and how to manage his money. After leaving boxing, he opened a highly successful restaurant and bar in New York's Times Square. Customers thronged Jack Dempsey's restaurant, knowing that their genial host would cheerfully greet them, sign autographs, and pose for pictures. A favorite pose was a smiling champ delivering a sham knockout blow to his happy customer's jaw. Dempsey's second career was every bit as successful as his years in the ring. He died on May 31, 1983, at the age of eighty-seven.

His spirit lives on in his boyhood home. Many a fan of the champ, pausing in his museum to reflect on Jack Dempsey's career, has had a sudden image of a misty fist surging towards him, only to have the blow dissolve in the air before striking. The gentleman host aspect of Jack Dempsey's spirit has struck again.

UFOs over Colorado

The San Luis Valley in south-central Colorado has proven to be a hot spot for UFO sightings. Even before the European discovery of the Americas, the local Native Americans were in awe of the paranormal reputation of the area. Hunting expeditions in that valley and the nearby Sangre de Cristo Mountains were carried out by large groups of hunters; lone hunters, or even small bands, regularly went missing, never to be seen again. Some ancient legends described mysterious "balls of fire" that zoomed through the skies there, sometimes hovering briefly as though curiously examining a village or campsite.

While UFO flaps—repeating sightings in the same area, witnessed by scores or even hundreds of people—are not really rare, they do seem to occur frequently in the San Luis Valley. One theory advanced by some ufologists is that UFOs can access a vast labyrinth of underground tunnels and bases. One of the suspected portals to these subterranean refuges is Blanca Peak, a 14,345-foot-high mountain near the southern end of the Sangre de Cristo range and the San Luis Valley.

Representative of the many UFO incidents in the vicinity is the rash of sightings near the little community of Crestone, as reported by the *Crestone Eagle*'s Chris O'Brien in April 1993. "White-gold" laser lights distinguished the fast-moving discs that were observed by many locals. The mysterious craft, able to maneuver at incredibly high speeds, were reported to the state police. Jet fighters from Peterson Air Force Base near Colorado Springs scrambled to pursue the UFOs, apparently without success. The Air Force allegedly claimed to have sent fighters to the area on a "routine training flight."

There have been plenty of other sightings of supposed UFOs in the Colorado skies. On July 7, 1947, a farmer driving a hay baler in a field east of Greeley observed three saucer-like craft flying in a complicated, zigzag pattern, combining incredible speed with impossibly sharp turns. As the farmer watched, one of the strange craft began to falter, losing speed and altitude. The other two objects seemed to flank their stricken colleague and closely escort it to the south, with all three craft slowing down and maintaining a straight-line course. The next day, July 8, the first reports appeared concerning the infamous Roswell incident, an alleged discovery of the wreckage of a UFO. Roswell, New Mexico, lies about 450 miles almost due south of Greeley. Did the impaired UFO seen over Greeley become the downed wreck near Roswell?

In the 1970s a string of cattle mutilations was linked to UFO appearances, at least in the minds of many ranchers. Night after night, cattle were found dead on pasture, with their udders, sex organs, and eyes missing. Police patrols and groups of armed ranchers failed to identify any suspicious vehicles in the neighborhood. Was it just coincidence that flurries of UFO reports occurred on those same evenings? Was there an attempted cover-up by the government in an effort to head off a public panic over UFO-related, systematic mutilations? The wounds on the unfortunate animals were not ragged or uneven as would happen if they had been victimized by predators. And why was all the blood drained from the cattle? What predator would leave such clean, precise wounds? Men claiming to be government veterinarians assured ranchers that the damage had been caused by coyotes. "Yeah," said one experienced rancher, "Real smart coyotes. Coyotes who use scalpels!"

If, as many assume, the UFOs are piloted by visiting extraterrestrials, are these tourists from outer space interested in the human history of earth? There have been reports of unidentified flying objects over the famed archeological sites of Colorado's southwestern area. There, many thousands of Native Americans once built cliff dwellings like Mesa Verde, Hovenweep, and the stone structures in the Canyon of the Ancients such as Lowry Pueblo. The alien tourists, if indeed that is what or who they are, are most likely to visit the ruins on moonlit nights. The UFOs are described as hovering over the ruins at low altitudes for several minutes, then zooming quickly away. Too bad the National Park Service has not figured out a way to collect admission fees.

The Shade of the Swashbuckler

The opera house in Central City was built in 1878. This magnificent Victorian building still functions as a theater, hosting an annual opera season and holding tours of the opulent auditorium, the backstage, and even the dressing rooms. These tours are deservedly popular, even if the ghosts don't make an appearance. Phantoms have been seen at various locations in the 550-seat theater, on the stage itself, and even in the dressing rooms.

Two ghosts in particular stand out amongst the small spectral army of former patrons, actors, stagehands, and cleaning staff reported over the years: Oscar Wilde and Douglas Fairbanks Sr. Two more radically different men, or rather ghosts, could hardly be imagined.

The spirit of English author, playwright, and well-known sophisticate Oscar Wilde is the older of these two ghosts. Oscar appeared in person when the opera house and Central City were both new and boisterously successful. Much of Central City had burned down in 1874, including the town's wooden opera house. The opera house was rebuilt in stone, a material rarely used in the mining towns. The newly rich miners were determined to flaunt their recently acquired veneer of culture and sophistication. A splendid opera house was the perfect expression of their wistful pursuit of culture and respectability. They even attended actual operas, performed by highly paid stars from the East Coast and Europe. Illiterate but very lucky former thugs now sought to act like gentlemen.

Still, some newly rich ex-ruffians felt that their manners might not quite measure up to the highest standards, and so touring lecturer Oscar Wilde was booked to give his views on cosmopolitan manners. Oscar personified pretentious, urbane elitism. He appeared onstage dressed in high, Victorian-era fashion: silk knee breeches, silk stockings, white patent-leather pumps with high heels, and a colorfully embroidered waistcoat over a frilly white shirt. His audience gaped as Wilde minced about the stage lecturing on deportment and dress. To this day, Oscar Wilde's phantom occasionally appears in his silks and frills, as outlandish still as he was in person.

The other famous ghost to show up on stage at the venerable opera house is that of Douglas Fairbanks Sr. On screen, Fairbanks portrayed the adventurous, athletic, self-confident hero, willing to take huge risks to frustrate evil and rescue the beautiful damsel in distress. He singlehandedly invented and perfected a whole genre of adventure films—the swashbuckler.

While Oscar Wilde's appearance in the opera house occurred at the height of his career, Douglas Fairbanks's performances there were as a neophyte actor at the beginning of an illustrious career. Fairbanks was born Douglas Ullman in Denver on May 23, 1883. His father abandoned his family when Douglas was only five, and his mother went back to using her first husband's name, Fairbanks.

Young Douglas aspired to be an actor and got his start in summer stock in Central City, Leadville, and Denver.

Fairbanks's early films (his first was in 1916) were comedies—he had a gift for humor that carried through on his later adventure spectaculars. He co-wrote the screenplays for two of his most successful films, *Robin Hood* (1923) and *The Black Pirate* (1926). Throughout the 1920s, when he made nine of his nineteen films, he and his first wife Mary Pickford were the second- and third-highest paid film stars (Charlie Chaplin was number one). Fairbanks was elected as the first president of the Motion Picture Academy of Arts and Sciences in 1927, the same year that he and Mary Pickford were the first to leave their hand- and footprints in fresh cement at Graumann's Chinese Theater in Hollywood.

Fairbanks was a great athlete who did his own stunts. His last great swashbuckler, *Mister Robinson Crusoe* was made when he was fifty; he was still in fine condition. His career was fading though, and movie offers were fewer and unappealing. In 1934, he made his last film, *The Private Life of Don Juan*. It was a bomb, panned by critics and shunned by audiences. Fairbanks had aged visibly and his once-trim figure had sagged. The onetime undisputed king of Hollywood was despondent and ignored. After five years of inactivity, he decided to go on a strict diet and exercise vigorously, trying to regain his "swashbuckling" figure. His cardiologist had advised against strenuous exercise but Fairbanks was determined to restart his career. He died of a heart attack at age 56; his last words were "I've never felt better in my life."

Fortunately for those who glimpse his ghost onstage in Central City's restored opera house, his spirit is in the form of the handsome, dashingly active young man at the dawn of a fabulous career. No one did swashbucklers like Douglas Fairbanks, a true American original and now a captivating spirit.

Through the Tunnel of Death

Snow can be either very good news or very bad news, depending on one's point of view. For operators of ski resorts, snow is white gold. They pray for it, and they smile in blizzards. For Colorado Railroad workers, snow is the enemy. Snow costs money to remove from the tracks. Heavy snowfalls wreak havoc with schedules.

Too much snow was the motivation for building the Moffat Tunnel. More than six miles in length, it is the second-longest railroad tunnel in the United States. Located about fifty miles west of Denver, the Moffat Tunnel is more than two thousand feet lower than the Berthoud Pass across the Continental Divide, the former pinnacle of the Denver–Salt Lake route.

The tunnel was the dream of David Moffat, a Denver banker who well understood the economic importance of Denver's location on a main transcontinental railroad. The easier grade across the Rockies lay in Wyoming, west of Cheyenne. If Denver was to remain the most important city along the Rocky Mountain front, it had to be on an important transcontinental railroad.

The Moffat Tunnel, twenty-four feet high and eighteen feet wide, was an engineering challenge that ended up costing eighteen million dollars instead of the original estimate of seven million. Today, the tunnel is a point of interest along the Denver–Salt Lake City leg of Amtrak's *California Zephyr* route. Not all the passengers bother to look out the windows during the tunnel transit. Some who do see ghosts.

Twenty-eight men died digging the tunnel. Many believe that their spirits remain in the tunnel that killed them. The reason for the high death rate, and for the huge cost overrun, was the nature of the rock under James Peak. It was assumed that the mountain was solid granite. It wasn't. As the tunnel progressed, engineers discovered that the core of the mountain was not tough granite but muddy shale—a weak, crumbly rock with little integrity. Roof collapses were a continual nightmare. The tunnel required almost continuous shoring-up, a tedious and expensive process. Cave-ins killed as many as six men at one time. The tunnel took four years to complete. An average of four workers died for every mile completed.

Some tunnel workers died almost instantly in cave-ins. Tons of rock falling on them quickly crushed them to a bloody pulp. A moment of unbelievable pain, and it was over. For others, death came agonizingly slowly. Falling rock knocked them flat, often breaking bones and tearing great gashes in now-helpless bodies. The rock debris and mounds of dust cut off their air supply. Their laboring lungs drew in only gritty dust. They died with the certain and terrible knowledge of approaching doom. Their faces, contorted in pain, horror, and fear, are the most terrible of the phantoms that haunt the Moffat Tunnel.

The railroad workers who regularly passed through the Moffat learned to look straight ahead like the locomotive's headlight, ignoring the fleeting glimpses of mind-numbing horror alongside the rails. Those ghostly forms and phosphorescent faces are both terrifying and supremely sad. It is best to pretend that they are not there, that they couldn't be there.

Most passengers on the *Zephyr* notice nothing, having quickly concluded that staring out the window at total darkness holds zero interest. But for some, an occasional, absent-minded glance produces a jolt of adrenaline from glimpsing a momentary image of faces frozen in terrible agony. Did they actually see what they thought they saw? Could they have seen, for a startling microsecond, the eerily glowing outlines of tunnel diggers at the moments of their long-ago deaths? Some passengers swear that they broke into cold sweats at their brush with the tortured ghosts of the tunnel. Tourists making a round trip on the *California Zephyr* have been known to clamp their eyes shut on their second transit of the Moffat Tunnel, the tunnel of death.

Shades of the Railroad War

The ghosts of the railroad men work feverishly at their tasks. Oddly, it is late at night. Scores of kerosene lamps lined up along the right-of-way illuminate hundreds of workers toiling in the narrow gorge. They move quickly, their muscles flexing under their sweaty shirts. Gleaming steel rails and heavy timber ties seem to fly in the hands of the determined men. But something very odd is going on. Not only are these phantoms, and not only is the action taking place late at night, but they are not laying track. Quite the opposite. They are tearing up track—demolishing rather than building.

Allegedly, this spectral scene is reenacted on summer nights with a full moon, recalling the events of July 1875. The scene is the bottom of the spectacular Royal Gorge, more than a thousand feet deep and, in some places, only thirty feet wide. This gorge was cut by the Arkansas River as it snaked its way through the Rocky Mountains and on across the Great Plains. As scenery, the gorge is awesome. As a route for a railroad, it was plainly impossible, or so said the first surveyors to travel through it. Nonetheless, the railroad was built. In fact, it was built, demolished, rebuilt, torn up again, and rebuilt yet again in the "railroad war" that the ghosts refight every July.

The story is that the Denver and Rio Grande Railroad had reached Cañon City but there was no sign of the company's intentions to continue westward through the gorge. At the time, there was a bitter rivalry between the Denver and Rio Grande and the Santa Fe Railroads. Both railroads wanted to control the route through the Rockies offered by the Arkansas River but neither was in a hurry to confront the engineering challenges of the deep and narrow slot-like gorge.

Landowners and entrepreneurs in Cañon City were frustrated. Surely money would flow into town as the railroad was built, and Cañon City would be on a main line to the Southwest, even the Pacific Ocean. Something had to be done. Local investors organized the Cañon City and San Juan Railroad and made surveys, which were duly filed with the federal government. That got the attention of both the Denver and Rio Grande and the Santa Fe Railroads. Each company promptly dispatched crews of workers to the entrance of the gorge. The Denver and Rio Grande crew beat their Santa Fe rivals by half an hour. They already were grading their right-of-way when the Santa Fe team arrived, and the "war" began. Each team laid rails by day and tore up the rails of the enemy by night. This being an intense competition between rough-and-ready, hardworking and hard-drinking brawlers, guns were produced. A lot of money was at stake. Many shots were fired but, somehow, no one was killed. Eventually, the dispute was settled by the courts. The Denver and Rio Grande won the right to build through Royal Gorge, and only the ghosts are still at war.

The Spirits of Grand Lake

Grand Lake lies on the western edge of the Rocky Mountain National Park amid magnificent scenery. It is very deep, very cold, and very beautiful. It is also very haunted, and for good reason. One of the largest lakes in the state, Grand Lake was formed thousands of years ago, when a great glacier dumped rock debris across the upper valley of the Colorado River. The Ute Indians placed great value on the area because of its outstanding hunting and fishing—at least until the massacre.

Colorado's Indian tribes were at war with one another almost continuously. The Ute were the mountain dwellers, while the Cheyenne, Arapaho, Comanche, Kiowa, and Pawnee were people of the plains. The Cheyenne and Arapaho usually were allied against the Comanche and Kiowa, but the longest and most bitter wars were those that pitted the mountain Indians against the plains Indians.

The Ute vigorously defended the mountain passes that could be used by invading plains tribes. For the Ute, any incursion of plains Indians into their mountains was a declaration of war. Many centuries ago, an overwhelming force of Cheyenne and Arapaho penetrated the Ute's mountain fortress along the shore of Grand Lake. The lake was deep in the heart of Ute territory; they should have had ample warning of invaders from the plains, but they didn't.

Over the years, many claim to have glimpsed the ghostly reenactments of the stealthy attack on the Ute village at Grand Lake. The most likely times to witness this gruesome reprise are said to be on spring nights with full moons. The attackers, unfamiliar with the local terrain, need just enough light to move into their enemy's camp. Strangulation is the preferred method of killing. The phantoms of Ute warriors die again just as silently as they did the first time, their eyes bulging out of their sockets as the strong cords twisted around their necks tighten and cut deeply into the flesh. Their entire bodies contort as they writhe in agony; the ghostly images themselves appear to shift from greenish-white to blood red.

According to Ute legend, the attackers fell back into the trees as the alarm spread and the defenders valiantly reacted. The Cheyenne and Arapaho pulled back temporarily to conserve their strength for the main part of the battle, which everyone knew would be a battle to the death. No mercy was shown and none was expected. The Cheyenne and Arapaho, having already dispatched one in five of the Ute braves in the initial assault, fired their arrows from the cover of the trees.

The Ute took advantage of this lull in fighting to lash logs together to form a large raft. Women and children were placed on the raft for their safety and pushed out on to the lake to await their fate. A Cheyenne victory would lead to the slaughter of most of the Ute women and children. Comely maidens and young children would be kidnapped into slavery. Some slaves might be traded to other tribes, and some ransomed back to the Ute.

Then, as recorded in legend, the already horrific day for the Ute evolved into a total disaster. Dark, roiling clouds rolled quickly in from the west. Thunder rolled like giant war drums. The terrified women and children were helpless, with no way to control the raft. The raft drifted to the center of Grand Lake, where it was capsized by the fierce winds of the rising storm. On shore, the Cheyenne and Arapaho renewed their attack with reinvigorated ferocity. They were convinced that the gods of the sky and storms chose to support their side. The remaining Ute warriors were cut down in a hail of arrows, the wounded clubbed to death.

In Ute tradition, Grand Lake is forever cursed. The mists rising from its waters are the spirits of the drowned women and children. Swimmers who brave the icy waters may feel a little tug on their feet as the doomed souls reach out desperately for help. Stay out of Grand Lake; blame the cold temperatures for your wise decision not to swim there. Watch the mists rising from the lake. Can't you see the spirits of the dead?

Southern Plains

THIS REGION LIES IN COLORADO'S SOUTHEAST CORNER. KANSAS BOUNDS it to the east, and Oklahoma and New Mexico lie to the south. Interstate 70 forms the northern boundary; the Rockies lie to the west. The region's important cities and towns include Colorado Springs, Pueblo, Walsenburg, and Trinidad.

Here you'll encounter the victims of a massacre and some truly scary headless ghosts. An alleged petrified man is the focus of one tale. The ghost of Kit Carson will invite you to decide whether this controversial man was a hero or a ruthless, genocidal killer.

Don't Say Macbeth

They say that ghosts are more likely to appear in areas or buildings where strong emotional or psychic energies are concentrated. These pools of human emotions linger, attracting and supporting spirits. For these reasons, theaters are common venues for ghosts.

The auditorium of Palmer High School in Colorado Springs is said to be haunted by an angry, frustrated, and vengeful ghost. Allegedly, this is the spirit of a student, a would-be actress who was denied a role in the school production of *Macbeth*. Brokenhearted, the despondent girl hanged herself in the women's restroom just behind the stage. This is said to have occurred in the

1960s. Her name has been forgotten, but some students over the years have called her Mona, after the mysterious moaning sounds sometimes heard backstage and in the restroom.

According to the story, "Mona" was fascinated by live theater. She envisioned herself as a glamorous star and decided to begin her no-doubt skyrocketing career in high school plays. To her great dismay, she was not given the female lead in the first production after she joined the school's theater club. She was politely but firmly advised that no one started at the top, not even beautiful, ambitious, and very, very pushy young ladies. She needed to acquire some experience. Mona was told to begin her arduous climb to the pinnacles of show business by showing up at all rehearsals and watching others work. She was also told that she would benefit from learning the fundamentals of all the theater crafts. She should volunteer to paint scenery, keep track of props, assist the actors with their costumes, and learn the rudiments of stage makeup.

Mona threw her considerable energies into becoming indispensable backstage. By the close of her first season, she was being rewarded with walk-on bit parts, even a line or two. She looked forward to her second year with the theater club. Surely, as a seasoned veteran and cooperative jack-of-all-trades, she was ready for the big time. The first play on the calendar was Shakespeare's classic, *Macbeth*. Mona just knew that she'd be a perfect Lady Macbeth. She understood that character's motivation, as she too was driven by overreaching ambition.

She didn't get the part. The classmate who won the role sneered that Mona should practice her cackle and try out for one of the witches, telling her, "You'd be a natural for a witch." Her fury matched only by her disappointment, Mona hanged herself in the restroom to which she'd retreated to cry her heart out. Mona's last thoughts were of vengeance. She'd show them. Thus began the haunting.

Small props would disappear. Or, worse yet, they would fall noisily to the floor while the play was in progress. Freshly painted backdrops would be found the next morning covered in flat black paint; costumes would be found cut to pieces. In the restroom in which Mona had drawn her last painful breath, unexplained crying and moaning sounds became common events.

It became part of Palmer High's folklore that just saying *Macbeth* on stage would produce a storm of mishaps: Lights would go out, microphones malfunctioned, props flew off tables, and actors would trip and fall onstage. The school never again planned a production of *Macbeth*. It became a tradition that the last person to leave the stage would say "Goodbye Mona. Sleep well." This seemed to calm the malevolent spirit. Everyone hopes that Mona, or whatever her name was, eventually will move on to the spirit world. Just remember not to say "Macbeth" out loud in Palmer High's auditorium. Someone or something might hear you.

The Schizophrenic Ghost

Either Kit Carson's ghost is schizophrenic or those who see it are projecting their own strong opinions of the man onto the blank canvas of his misty outline. Either way, the ghost reflects the controversy at the center of any attempt to understand Kit Carson.

Both the positive and negative versions of Carson's ghost share the same general physical description. Kit's phantom appears as the once-living person did in late middle age. He is dressed plainly but neatly in a black suit and white shirt. He is not wearing a tie because, as he used to say, ties reminded him of a hangman's noose, and he'd seen many men hanged, some thanks to his own strict interpretation of the law. Kit is wearing a neatly trimmed mustache but no beard. His thin hair is combed across his balding head. He looks rather ordinary, neither a superhero nor a mass murderer—until the supernatural image focuses his eyes on his beholder. Then, reflecting the prejudices or preconceptions of the witness, either Kit's ghost radiates courage, honesty, and determination fused with integrity, or he projects a demonic bloodlust for ruthless genocide.

Few were neutral about Kit Carson in his lifetime. People tended to either admire him as an American hero, or detest him as a man of blood and violence, undeterred by thoughts of mercy or sympathy for his victims. When either version of his spirit shows up, it is usually in the cabin in which he died back in 1868. Now the Kit Carson Museum, the cabin is located in the little town of Las Animas in southeastern Colorado. Carson was buried nearby at Fort Lyon beside his third wife, who had died only a month before her husband. Later, both Kit and his wife were dug up and reburied at Taos, New Mexico, his wife's family home. It is possible that Kit Carson's ghost haunts the place of his death because it was disturbed and annoyed by the disinterment from his first grave. As many a Native American knew, it was not a good idea to annoy Kit Carson.

Christopher "Kit" Carson was born in Kentucky on Christmas Eve, 1809, and grew up in Missouri. At the age of sixteen, he decided he wanted some adventure in his life and left home to join a wagon train on the Santa Fe Trail. He didn't bother telling his parents where he was heading. Kit became a frontier scout of renown, a trapper and trader, a teamster, and a cook; he even tried his hand at surgery, removing a man's gangrenous arm when nobody else had the nerve to do it.

He killed his first Indian, an Apache, when he was twenty years old, but he definitely was not of the "only good Indian is a dead Indian" school of thought. He often expressed sympathy and admiration for Indians. He tried hard to communicate with them and became fluent in Navajo, Ute, Cheyenne, and Arapaho. His first wife, a Ute, died young after giving birth to their daughter. His second wife, a Cheyenne, was extravagant with Kit's money and threw him out of their house in an "Indian-style divorce," as Kit put it. His third wife, Josefa, a wealthy Hispanic, was the sister-in-law of the governor of New Mexico. When he married her, she was fourteen and he was thirty-four. They had eight children together. She died of childbirth complications only a month before he passed away.

Kit Carson's work as an Indian agent brought him to the height of his fame or notoriety, depending on your viewpoint. Indian agents were federal officials, a kind of overseer, negotiator, and captor in charge. Kit followed orders, even if he believed those orders were unduly harsh. Kit tried to understand the Indian viewpoint and recognized that the whites often were the first to break treaties and use savage violence. He once said in defense of Indians, "Indians in their outrages were only imitating or improving on the white man's bad example." The Indians respected the fact that he bothered to learn their languages and that he never lied to them.

When the Civil War broke out, Carson became a colonel in the Union army. The Navajo increased their raids, taking advantage of the withdrawal of most soldiers to the east. Carson warned them that he must force them onto a reservation. He waged a ruthless economic war on them, burning their crops and slaughtering the animals on which they depended. He offered food only if they surrendered to him. Thousands died of starvation before most Navajo turned themselves in and agreed to a peace treaty. Was Kit Carson guilty of racial holocaust or was he attempting to minimize bloodshed? His policies remain as controversial today as they were in his lifetime. Which of his ghostly personas is the more accurate?

Bent's Old Fort's Old Ghosts

Bent's Old Fort National Historic Site is an exact reproduction of the adobe trading post that stood on this site between 1833 and 1849. The reconstruction is so convincingly accurate that the ghosts of the original fort's inhabitants evidently feel right at home, at least according to many tourists and a few staff who wish to remain anonymous.

The historic site is located six miles east of La Junta. Daily tours are available; ghost sightings or sensings are not everyday occurrences. Bent's Old Fort played an important role in Colorado's early history as it was as the juncture ("La Junta") of the main and southern paths of the Santa Fe Trail, a major trade route. That portion of the Santa Fe Trail that crossed through what is now Colorado followed the Arkansas River. At Bent's Old Fort the southern route branched off, heading southwest for the Raton Pass down into New Mexico.

The post was founded by brothers William and Charles Bent. The brothers knew that trading with the Indians was a potentially hazardous occupation, not to mention the threat of being robbed by frontier bandits. Their fort was a heavily fortified trading post where traders, trappers, plainsmen, Indians, soldiers, and adventurers of all ethnicities could trade and rest in security. At its height, one hundred men were employed at Bent's Old Fort and it was the most important trading post for hundreds of miles.

The fort was impressive. It was 180 feet long and 135 feet wide, with adobe walls fifteen feet high and four feet thick. Thirty-foot-high towers stood at the northwest and southwest corners. The walls and guard towers were constantly patrolled by armed guards, muskets at the ready. It is said that, day and night, guards stationed in the towers held burning matches close to small cannons, prepared to fire on short notice. Spiny cacti, nature's own razor wire, were planted atop the mud-brick walls, where they flourished. Vigilance was never relaxed at Bent's Old Fort, and the facility was never attacked.

Traveling the Santa Fe Trail and bargaining all day could make a man mighty thirsty. The Bent brothers thoughtfully provided a bar equipped with a billiard table, dispensing "Taos Lightning," a potent homemade whiskey. The old barroom is said to be one of the most haunted areas of the reconstructed fort. There are those who swear they've heard the sounds of a popular drinking ceremony reverberate in the otherwise quiet and empty bar. The object, apparently, was to get drunk as quickly as possible, all in unison. Thick, heavy glasses were used. "Charge the glasses!" was the order, meaning to fill the glasses to the brim with liquor. "Salute!" meant to raise the glass at arm's length. "Prepare to fire!" brought the glass to the lips. At "Fire!" the glass was to be drained in one swallow. "Stand down!" resulted in slamming one's empty glass down on the table. Supposedly, this routine was repeated until the participants couldn't remember the sequence of "orders." The well-orchestrated, simultaneous slamming of empty glasses on the bar or on tables seems to echo in the room very late at night. Are the ghosts of long-ago traders and trappers reliving some of their happiest moments at Bent's Old Fort?

The bar isn't the only venue for the spirits of the fort. Allegedly, faintly flickering lights sometimes can be seen in the guard towers. Are these just modern nightlights or are ghostly sentries still holding matches at the ready, prepared to fire their cannons at the first sign of trouble?

Legend has it that the ghosts of Bent's Old Fort will never trouble the living as long as they are properly saluted with liquor. Remember to use heavy glasses that won't shatter when slammed down. Salute!

Phantoms of a Massacre

The infamous Sand Creek Massacre location now is an official national historic site, but don't expect to find it well publicized. It is a memorial to a shameful and bloody incident in the history of Colorado. Basically, it is not well advertised because we are ashamed of what happened there back on November 29, 1864. Maybe it is just as well that the site has relatively few visitors, for it is said to be haunted by specters that are both pathetic and frightening. These ghosts are bitterly angry and, perhaps justifiably, vengeful.

Sand Creek Massacre National Historic Site is roughly seven miles north of the little town of Chivington on Route 96, about twenty-six miles west of the Kansas line. It is an unremarkable section of Colorado's dry, high plains—except for the Indian blood that once saturated its rich soil and stained the conscience of a nation.

The best (or maybe the worst) time to encounter the ghosts of those slain in the massacre is late November, around dawn. The ghosts are said to be hyperactive at times—old men, women, and children running frantically away from the blue-coated soldiers firing at them with rifles and howitzers. At other times, the shades of bullet-riddled Indians seem to move in slow motion, mouths open in silent screams, as they flee the terrible violence. No one can be sure how many died that morning. Estimates range from 150 to five hundred. The encampment is believed to have been made up of a mixture of Cheyenne and Arapaho. The Indians always claimed, and in time many whites came to agree, that the Sand Creek Camp was made up of peaceful women, children, and old men with no warriors to protect them. The army's decision to attack may have been based on faulty intelligence within a general atmosphere of fear on the part of the whites. Whatever the motives for it, the unprovoked slaughter was horrific. No wonder that many people have alleged that the ghosts of the massacre seem bent on revenge, making hostile gestures toward those brave enough to visit the massacre site.

At the time of the massacre, naked, harrowing fear had been the constant companions of Colorado's white citizens for four long years. At the beginning of the nation's Civil War, the soldiers who had kept the peace on the plains were withdrawn back east. Many tribes took advantage of this situation to rise up again to reclaim their lost hunting grounds. Wagon trains were attacked and settlers murdered. The Santa Fe Trail was closed to travel on several occasions. The territorial governor called a peace parley at Fort Lyon, where the Cheyenne and Arapaho agreed to give up all lands east of the mountains and lying between the Arkansas and Platte Rivers in return for $450,000 to be paid over a period of five years. But the federal government failed to deliver the money, leaving those tribes on the verge of starvation. Indian raids resumed with a vengeance.

Colonel John Chivington took charge. Chivington decided that enough was enough—the hostile Indians must be dealt with quickly and firmly. In imitation of his hero, Gen. Ulysses S. Grant, he said that his policy was to "Attack, attack, and attack until the enemy is beaten."

Chivington was told that a large number of hostile Indians had set up camp on Sand Creek (now called Big Sandy River) and were plotting to attack white settlers. The colonel decided on making a preemptive strike with his 750 soldiers. He ordered that no prisoners be taken. When the killing was over, the village was burned. Chivington later claimed that his men had been incensed by the sight of the scalps hanging from teepees, but of course the fires destroyed that evidence.

News of the controversial massacre quickly spread. The U.S. Senate created an investigative committee that recommended a court martial for Chivington, but he was never brought to trial. He continued to maintain that those killed at Sand Creek were mostly hostile warriors and that most women and children escaped unharmed. The town nearest the massacre site still bears his name.

The Headless Phantoms of Pueblo

Most people would agree that ghosts are seldom a happy sight. As benign as some apparitions might be, their appearances are disturbing rather than reassuring. Some phantoms are just downright scary, even if they themselves are the spirits of slaughtered innocents and not evil in history or intent. The most horrible visions of the supernatural are those stemming from senseless, vicious murders. The victims of unprovoked, violent mutilation become ghosts that are at the same time pitiable and fearsome.

Pueblo is inhabited, if that's the word, by many spirits from many incidents. But the ones that are the most likely to sear their images into the memories of the unfortunate beholders are the headless ghosts of the Christmas Eve Massacre.

The little trading settlement of Pueblo already was a dozen years old in 1854, and the most important place in the area before the gold rush days. Although trade with the Native Americans had proceeded fairly peaceably for more than a decade, the trading center was also a fort, a large square area surrounded by adobe walls. Many emigrants passing through on the way to California stopped to rest and reprovision here in the valley of the Arkansas River.

Among the more popular trade goods available at Pueblo was a particularly potent whiskey known as Taos Lightning. Taos Lightning was made in the New Mexico village of that name and was famous far and wide among frontiersmen. Superlatives abound in the various descriptions of Taos Lightning: It was the strongest whiskey, the best-tasting whiskey, the worst-tasting whiskey, the drink most likely to foster erotic dreams, the booze most likely to induce uncontrollable tremors, and the libation most useful in courting lovely ladies. There was unanimous agreement that Taos's finest produced the most persistent and violent hangovers.

Like other alcoholic beverages, Taos Lightning evidently had the capacity to dissolve clear thinking among its abusers. The local Utes had been behaving suspiciously in late 1854, displaying uncharacteristic sullenness. Famous frontiersman "Uncle Dick" Wooton operated a ranch near Pueblo, and he strongly advised his neighbors to keep the fort's gates closed and guarded, not allowing Indians inside. But it was Christmas Eve and every adult in Pueblo was brimming with goodwill, cheer, and Taos Lightning. Drunks threw open the fort's gates and invited the Indians to the party. The revelry came to an abrupt end as the Utes' war clubs and axes were swung into action. Only two women, two children, and one old man, Romaldo, survived the orgy of blood. The murdered were decapitated so that their heads could be displayed at the victory celebration later. Romaldo was spared because the Indians were amused by his efforts to talk with a bullet lodged in his tongue.

The spirits of the Christmas Eve Massacre victims appear only briefly, a blessing for their witnesses. They are seen running in panic, directionless due to their missing heads. Blood gushes from their necks. They fall down, limbs still twitching. Understandably, living observers of this horror have been known to pass out.

The phantom of Uncle Dick Wooton is much less horrifying than the headless ones. Uncle Dick shows up now and then in local bars around Pueblo. His misty figure has a friendly smile just before it disappears. In life, Uncle Dick was a pioneer scout, sheepherder of renown (he once herded 9,000 sheep across the desert from New Mexico to California, losing only a hundred along the trail), and legendary trader. His trades always proved profitable to him, possibly thanks to his custom of offering free drinks all around from a barrel of Taos Lightning before beginning negotiations. Uncle Dick made a fortune by building a tollgate across Raton Pass, south of Trinidad, once a major north-south trade route. Some claim that his ghost will offer a free drink to anyone who looks like a possible trading partner.

A very interesting and nonthreatening ghost around Pueblo is the spirit of Don Romaldo, the only adult male survivor of the Christmas Massacre. In extreme old age, he became famous as a foreteller of the future. His tongue healed with the bullet still in it, a condition to which Romaldo credited his ability to speak of the future. Two of his predictions, made nearly a century and a half ago, are especially interesting.

For decades after the Christmas Eve Massacre, Pueblo was avoided by traders who swore they'd seen the headless ghosts. Romaldo was asked if the town would ever prosper again. Yes, he said, the place would grow mightily when fire was dug from the earth. Years later, he was proven correct: Pueblo became an important iron and steel center when coal mines were opened nearby.

Another frequent question for Romaldo was whether the Arkansas River would continue to flood the town. The seer, as he was called, replied that the floods would end when they built a new river, an unbelievable idea. In April 1921, a disastrous flood on the Arkansas swept away six hundred houses and killed several hundred people. In 1924, the Arkansas River was relocated to a concrete-lined channel. They had built a new river, just as Romaldo said they would. His ghost is said to walk along the river's concrete banks, gesturing and talking soundlessly. Too bad we can't get near him—he might be trying to tell us something about the future.

Thirteen O'Clock

Will listened carefully as the clock struck the hour. He had learned to pay close attention to the number of times the chimes tolled out the hours. He was certain the clock was bewitched. Why else would it strike thirteen, and why else would the thirteenth bong warn of impending disaster?

The clock could be heard from any room in the old house in Colorado Springs that Will had inherited from his parents. An only child, Will had grown up in the house, which was little changed from his childhood, even down to the furniture and knickknacks his mother had collected. The clock sat on the marble mantel of the unused fireplace in the seldom-occupied, stiffly formal parlor.

It was a handsome clock. It was not really an antique, as it was about fifty years old, the same age as Will. The wood cabinet had been carefully waxed and polished every month by Will's mom, a tradition that Will continued. The polished brass face of the clock was decorated by carved brass cherubs and a plate inscribed with *tempus fugit*, Latin for "time flees (away from us)."

According to Will's parents, the clock's first instance of striking thirteen occurred a little after eleven in the morning, mountain time, on November 22, 1963, shortly after they'd gotten the clock. As they soon learned, the mysterious thirteen chimes coincided with the assassination of President John F. Kennedy. At first, Will's parents rationalized that they had not actually heard a thirteenth hour struck. The clock's "Westminster chimes" had already become so familiar that they were not always conscious of hearing them. They had simply misremembered the hours struck that morning, their memories distorted by the national trauma occasioned by the assassination. They couldn't have heard the clock strike thirteen— not only the most unlucky number, but one impossible for a clock of their type. The clock shop's owner, a talented repairman, pro- vided assurance that the clock's solid brass mechanism was in per- fect working order. It could not have struck thirteen, they were told; the clock's German design and craftsmanship were impeccable.

Several years went by without any extraordinary chimes from the clock. Then, late one night as Will and his parents were dozing off, they heard thirteen distinct, loud bongs. Here we go again, they thought. Shortly thereafter, the phone rang. It was the hospital where Will's grandfather was recovering from surgery. He had suffered a fatal stroke. This time, the clock had noted a personal rather than national tragedy.

A few months afterward, Will was awakened by an unearthly scream from his parents' bedroom. He reached his mother's bedside in time to hear her last words whispered: "It's thirteen o'clock!" Her face was frozen in a grimace of pain and shock from a massive heart attack. Thirteen o'clock indeed.

The clock went on to report news of other personal and national disasters. Will learned to turn on the news radio station and brace himself for a phone call whenever he heard the thirteenth hour struck. This anticipation of terrible news was accompanied by the dreadful realization that the clock could well be sounding Will's own death knell.

Border Guards

Out on the high, dry plains of eastern Colorado, trees grow only along rivers. Trees being a rarity on the plains, people tend to take notice of them, especially large trees. When corpses are spotted, fastened high up in the trees, passersby really pay attention. More than a century and a half ago, it wasn't all that unusual to see dead people tied to high branches—but they were there for a surprising reason. According to some, the phantoms of these long-ago dead still appear from time to time, carrying out their vital duties. Meet the sentinel corpses of the Comanche.

The ghosts of those warriors who once stood guard along the borders of Comanche territory are there still. They are not always visible, nor can everyone see them. In legend, the dead always faced outward, their backs to the heart of Comanche land. Their sightless eyes stared at would-be challengers or invaders; their decaying bodies warned of the ferocity and determination of their living counterparts. "Stop!" they seemed to command. "Go no further. You have been warned!" they appear to shout in a silent scream.

The Comanche chose a unique role for their warriors who had been killed in battle. In death, they became border guards. They functioned on two levels to repel invaders. The gruesome presence of their dead bodies certainly got the attention of those approaching Comanche territory—a deterrent as effective as any physical fortress would have been. On the spiritual level, the spirits of the deceased were said to be able to summon up the dark forces from the land of the dead. The long-departed ancestors of the Comanche could rise up in defense of their descendents. Hell's fury would be focused on the attackers.

The ghosts of these guardian corpses allegedly appear in the remote, almost empty lands along Highway 160 between Trinidad and the tiny settlement of Kim. This area once was contested by the Comanche and the Ute; the Comanche won, and they've kept it in the spiritual sense. Did the Comanche triumph because their unique border patrol was able to enlist the aid of the legions of the dead?

The compulsion to mark and defend territory is as old as humankind. Like many other creatures, people are territorial animals. It all comes down to the need to protect one's food supply. Add to that a related and strong instinct to defend the nest from intruders and you have the territorial assertiveness that motivates walls and fences and "no trespassing" signs. The dead Comanche warriors suspended in trees were dramatic "no trespassing" signs. To the Comanche, their dead, slain in battle, were being honored by being assigned to guard duty along the boundaries of the land which provided sustenance for the tribe.

Are those just random patterns of leaves blowing in the wind or are they the shadows of the Comanche border guards of the distant past? Was that a skull gleaming from that treetop? Were the dead simply supremely effective warnings against invaders or were they symbols of the enlistment of supernatural forces? Or both?

Satanic Dreams

The dreams had become so disturbing recently that Ann dreaded going to sleep. The dreams varied some in details but the main theme was constant. There would be a mounting sense of awareness of approaching danger, followed by a sudden, frenzied attack, and then unremitting pain and horror. In the previous evening's nightmare, a mountain lion had invaded the small apartment she had just moved into, relentlessly stalking her from room to room, quickly discovering each of her pathetic hiding places. There was no escaping the beast, which was smart and quick. It cornered her in the bathtub. The huge cat's greenish-yellow eyes, brimming with bloodlust, seemed to bore into her soul. She could smell its foul breath as it bared its gleaming ivory fangs. The cat then knocked her flat with a pounce, took her by the throat, and raked open her abdomen with the sharp claws of its hind feet.

And then Ann woke up. She was covered in an icy sweat. The front of her nightgown was in shreds. To her horror, her stomach was covered with deep, bleeding gashes that slowly healed and disappeared as she watched. Soon, the only physical evidence of her horrific experience was a torn nightgown. Was it just an unnervingly realistic, agonizingly painful dream? Had she ripped her own nightgown while thrashing about on her bed in the midst of the nightmare? Who could she tell? Who would believe her? Importantly, who would help her?

Ann hated to admit it, even to herself, but she knew in her heart that these nightmares were her own fault. She was lonely. She was a new arrival in Pueblo and new at her job as a fourth-grade schoolteacher. It had never been easy for her to make new friends. She spent a lot of time on her computer, fascinated by the infinite variety of websites. Bored and on a whim, she had begun typing in search requests for such topics as "Satan," "witchcraft," "demons," and "Hades."

Ann couldn't really remember how she stumbled onto a very scary website late one Saturday night. She had a somewhat hazy memory of typing in responses to questions about her belief in the devil and her willingness to serve him. How had she replied, if she'd replied? Had she accidentally found a site that was a very sinister one, or was it the first of her series of terrifying dreams?

She decided to confide in the pastor of the church she'd recently joined. He was about her age and she sensed a sympathetic interest in helping her. Was it possible that she actually had contacted the Devil, who now was visiting her in her home? Pastor Bryce, was well read on the subject of curses, witchcraft, and demons, all of which had fascinated him as a child. Bryce did not laugh off Ann's fears; indeed, he took them at face value. He suggested that, for the night, Ann should stay in the church, in a pew near the altar. She would sit literally surrounded by Bibles and prayer books. Bryce would stay in Ann's apartment to confront the Devil. The young man of God equipped himself with a Bible, a large wooden cross, and a toddler-sized plastic wading pool, along with a large supply of church candles.

He drew a pentagram, or five-pointed star, in chalk on Ann's living room rug, placing lit candles in each star point. Within the pentagram he placed the wading pool holding a few inches of water. In the pool was a chair in which he sat, holding his Bible and cross.

He didn't have to wait long that night. Evil materialized in the form of the mountain lion that had terrorized Ann. With a deep-throated growl, it circled the pentagram, and then launched itself in a leap aimed at the reverend. As the huge cat's body passed between the candles, fire shot out from the candles and consumed the unholy beast, which screamed in agony as it became a pile of black ash.

A large vulture was the next embodiment of all that is unholy. Its beak and talons glowed in the candlelight and its red eyes flashed like lightning. As it spread its wings in preparation for an attack, Bryce calmly held up the Bible before him. A laser-like burst of energy from the holy book struck the obnoxious bird, which promptly evaporated.

Finally, the Prince of Darkness showed up in human form. Perhaps fittingly, he was dressed like a Wall Street broker in an elegantly tailored, navy blue three-piece suit and scarlet silk tie. "Very clever of you," he complimented Reverend Bryce with a sinister smile. "Placing yourself within a pentagram and surrounded by water, which you know I hate to cross. I've come for Ann but I could take you instead." "You can't and you won't be back here, not ever," replied Bryce. "Why do you say that?" asked the Devil with a sneer. Bryce dipped the cross in the wading pool and then used it to shower the Devil with drops of water the reverend had blessed, just as he would have for a baptism. "This water is a symbol of eternal life, a gift of God, and it will burn you like Hell!" Satan yelped once in surprise and pain, and was gone in a puff of smoke.

Ann is no longer troubled by nightmares and no longer surfs the Internet looking for weird websites. Her new husband, Bryce, won't let her.

The Mysterious Muldoon

The rolling prairie country of Colorado's westernmost plains has many low ridges referred to by geologists as hogbacks. They are common and unremarkable, except that one, Muldoon Hill, fourteen miles southwest of Pueblo, was famous briefly for the astounding discovery there of a petrified man. Even more astounding is the legend of the petrified man's spirit, which is said to still roam the area late at night.

"Mysterious Muldoon" as he was advertised, was the allegedly petrified body of a presumably ancient human-like creature. The "stone man" was ten feet tall, and had been preserved in great anatomic detail, a fact that added to the prurient interest of the crowds that paid to view it. The arms were disproportionately long, and a rudimentary tail extended from the base of the spine. So as to not offend the sensibilities of the ladies, Muldoon was provided with an Indian-style loincloth.

The stone man's discoverer was William Conant, who called himself a geologist. He soon had the petrified giant on display in Pueblo at twenty-five cents a peek. The money rolled in as local "experts" agreed that this was not only real, but proof of the theory that people were related to apes. For the churchgoing disbelievers in evolution, Conant quoted Genesis 6:4, "There were giants on the earth in those days." "Come see the proof that Genesis is accurate!" said Conant.

Showman P. T. Barnum offered $20,000 for the Mysterious Muldoon but was turned down by Conant. Eventually, the stone man was revealed as a fraud. It has been fabricated from clay, plaster, and ground animal bones and baked in a furnace.

As it turned out, Mysterious Muldoon was but one of a rash of "petrified men" that had been "discovered" in many parts of the United States. They had all been inspired by the Cardiff Giant hoax. The Cardiff Giant had been unearthed by well diggers in Cardiff, New York, in 1869. It caused a sensation, earning a small fortune for its "discoverer," who later was found to have had it carved from a block of gypsum. The 1876 Muldoon Man, like the Cardiff Giant, was created by con artists taking advantage of the popular uproar caused by Charles Darwin's 1859 publication of *The Origin of Species*. Darwin was widely misquoted as asserting that humans were descended from monkeys—something he never said. The tail on the Muldoon Man was an inside joke on evolutionists.

The story doesn't end with the exposure of Mysterious Muldoon as a fake. People in the vicinity of Pueblo claim to have seen a living version of the stone man still roaming about. How could that be? The legend of William Conant's deathbed confession provides the answer. "Yes, I faked Muldoon Man to have a bit of fun and make some easy money," Conant is said to have admitted, "But I was inspired to make the stone man by my experience with Jackie."

Conant's story was that as a boy of ten, he was exploring Muldoon Hill by himself. A shy, unthreatening, immature Bigfoot-like creature appeared. Young William impulsively offered to share his food, which the animal accepted. For several years, Conant and his unlikely friend met briefly and shared snacks provided by the boy, who never told anyone about this, assuming no one would believe him. Conant claimed to have modeled his "petrified man" on the mysterious human-like creature of his acquaintance, exaggerating the height, adding a tail, and omitting the coarse hair, which, he reasoned, wouldn't turn to stone anyway.

"Why didn't you simply capture or kill the real creature and exhibit it?" asked a relative. "I'm not a monster with no morals!" retorted Conant. "I couldn't kill the inoffensive animal, nor would I lock a wild thing up in a cage for people to stare at." Does this original inspiration for the hoax, which sounds a great deal like contemporary descriptions of Bigfoot, still prowl Muldoon Hill and its neighborhood? Some are convinced that it is so, that there really is more to Mysterious Muldoon than just a fake stone man.

Western
Plateaus and Deserts

COMPOSING THE WESTERN THIRD OF COLORADO, THIS VERY LARGE region includes some of the least populated parts of the state. Some important towns in this region are Grand Junction, Glenwood Springs, Durango, and Montrose.

Some of this region's ghosts are ancient, such as those of Mesa Verde's Indian ruins. Others include the shades of Butch Cassidy and the Sundance Kid, who once hid in the nearly empty wilderness of the state's northwest corner. You'll encounter the ghost of an alleged cannibal and hear about a brush with Bigfoot. Readers will meet the legendary white burro; a UFO makes an appearance. A magical opal ring is also included in your tour of Colorado's "Wild West."

A Visit from Bigfoot

The Johnson family were experienced campers. They were in bear country, so they hoisted their knapsacks of food high up in a convenient tree. The canned goods were safe enough in camp, as not even bears can smell food through steel. The Johnsons were in a fantastically beautiful campsite just south of Spring Creek Pass along the continental divide. They had driven into Creede for supplies and to check out the tiny town's two museums. As they returned to camp, they witnessed a sight that they swear nearly stopped their hearts, burning an unforgettable image into their memories.

Just as they were arriving, their visitor was leaving. They glimpsed the back of the creature as it walked away—not in a panicked hurry but not wasting time, either. The creature was an impressive seven feet tall, covered in black or very dark brown fur. The animal was walking on its two hind legs and definitely was not a bear—they'd seen plenty of bears in their time and this was no bear. Bears will rear up on their hind legs to get a better view and to intimidate with their size, but they don't travel on two legs. Could they have seen a Bigfoot?

Inspection of the campsite seemed to provide proof that, yes, it was a Bigfoot. Food packed in cans that did not require a separate can opener—sardines, Spam, and corned beef—had been opened and eaten. Neatly. "Had to be a Bigfoot," observed the family expert, an anthropology major in her sophomore year at college. "Only monkeys and primates have opposable thumbs and manual dexterity."

They wondered if it would be back for another meal. Would it be aggressive toward them? The Johnsons built a larger campfire that night than was their custom. Sleep didn't come easily.

The next day the family drove up a nearby dirt road to explore the area of the Rio Grande's source. On return, they approached their campsite with caution, but it was empty. The "bear-proof" hanging knapsack also was empty of bags of marshmallows, while the pancake mix was untouched. "Bigfoot has a sweet tooth," commented their youngest. They were beginning to think of the camp raider as "their" Bigfoot. It had to be a Bigfoot, they all agreed. What else could it be?

That evening, as they relaxed around the dying fire just before crawling into their sleeping bags, they heard a twig snap from just outside the circle of firelight. The noise drew their attention to two glowing eyes watching them from the darkness. The eyes reflected a reddish radiance, much like the red-eye effect produced by camera flashbulbs in days past. The truly impressive part of this incident was the height of the eyes above the ground; the Johnsons estimated that the watcher's eyes were more than six feet above ground level.

Although the mysterious eyes quickly disappeared, the Johnsons got no sleep that night, and broke camp at first light. Had they really been visited by a Bigfoot? They are convinced that they were.

Bewitched by a UFO

Eli was evil. Maddie was convinced of it. Eli had entered her life as an appealing, affectionate kitten. The kitten was playful, endlessly curious, and sweet-natured—the ideal pet, thought Maddie. But that all ended with the UFO incident.

No one would have believed her anyhow, or at least that's how Maddie rationalized her decision not to report the UFO that she and Eli had encountered that day atop Iron Mountain. Maddie had gotten a blinding headache and recurring bad dreams from that horrible day. Eli fared worse—he was bewitched.

A lifelong resident of Glenwood Springs, thirty-year-old Maddie had never taken the glass-enclosed gondola ride to the top of Iron Mountain. That was something that tourists did. On a sparkling October day, however, she decided to ride the tramway. She tucked Eli into an oversized straw handbag in case animals were not welcomed. Eli was used to being smuggled into stores and restaurants in that manner and made no protest.

Maddie enjoyed the spectacular view of the Colorado River far below, so much so that she stayed behind at the observation area when the few other visitors went back down the mountain. She and Eli, now out of the bag and roaming about, would take a later gondola. She felt that she was on top of the world.

Suddenly, Maddie was aware that she was in shadow. The sun was bright, and the sky cloudless. How could she be in shadow? Alarmed, she looked directly above her. An enormous silver disk was hovering over her, perhaps a few hundred feet above the mountaintop. Maddie may have passed out for a few minutes—she's still not sure. In a dreamlike trance, she saw the unbelievable, the unexplainable. A narrow shaft of dazzlingly white light descended from the huge, hovering disk. It moved over Eli, who stood so still that he appeared frozen.

Slowly the little cat was drawn up into the belly of the spacecraft, as though on invisible wires. After what seemed a long time, although it was likely just a few minutes, Eli appeared again in the beam of light, slowly descending. His rigid body was not moving, not even a tail twitch. As the cat touched down, the light beam blinked out and the disk silently accelerated away, disappearing within seconds. Eli blinked, and then fell limp on the ground. Maddie placed him tenderly in her bag and took the next gondola down. No one else had witnessed the event.

Back home Eli slept for a solid twenty-four hours. When he awakened, he was an entirely different cat. He always had been independent and demanding, reminding Maddie of the old adage that "dogs had owners; cats had staff." But he had been affectionate in his way, and respectful of basic rules. For example, prior to their trip up Iron Mountain, Eli had been permitted to nap on Maddie's bed, provided that he stayed on a towel placed there for him. Now, Eli sprawled right on Maddie's own pillow, and hissed and growled menacingly when Maddie reached to move him. Eli began to jump up on the kitchen counter and help himself to food that Maddie was preparing for herself or guests. Such behavior had been strictly forbidden before. Now, Eli inflicted deep, painful scratches on Maddie as she reached to remove him.

It was clear that Eli was out of control. Maddie obtained some cat tranquilizer pills from the vet. As directed, she powdered them and mixed them into Eli's favorite dish of cubed fresh beef liver. Eli took one cautious bite, and then flew into a rage. He viciously bit Maddie on her ankles, then dashed to the door and demanded to be let out. Maddie was happy to see him leave. She never saw Eli again.

Meeker Is Not Better

Meeker is not better. No sir. Meeker is dead. He was killed in an Indian uprising back in 1879 but his spirit is said to still haunt the site of the Meeker Massacre, about ninety miles from the present-day town bearing his name. Meeker's ghost is restless and aggressive; his phantom is one you don't want to meet. He still is very angry that his murderers got away with the unprovoked slayings of eleven federal employees. Meeker believed himself and his colleagues to be the innocent victims of Indian treachery.

Nathan Meeker's ghost is a fearsome sight. Both arms are missing, hacked off by the steel axes that the Indians had acquired in trade. Great bloody gashes all over the body further testify to the sheer ferocity of the sudden attack. The phantom's eyes are unblinking and his mouth is open, contorted in an agonized scream that cannot be heard by the living.

Meeker was not particularly meek. Indeed, his offense against the Northern Utes, if any, was to zealously enforce the policies of the federal government. The policies may have been, in fairness to the Ute, culturally uninformed and a bit harsh. Washington bureaucrats had decided that the Ute must literally settle down. They were to give up their migratory way of life, following the movements of the animals they hunted. They were to be transformed overnight from hunters and gatherers to sedentary farmers and ranchers. The Ute were noticeably unenthusiastic about the fundamental change in their lives. The treaty that the Ute were coerced into signing promised the delivery of food to ease their transition to a new life, as well as farming tools. The promised aid never arrived.

In the meantime, Nathan Meeker, a well-known pioneer who had worked with Horace Greeley in establishing the agricultural colony at Greeley in 1870, was appointed Indian agent over the Northern Ute tribe. Meeker may have scored low on tact and diplomacy. He was unrelenting in his advocacy of federal directives. The Ute were sullen and restless.

Hearing of the turmoil at Meeker's Indian agency, three troops of cavalry were dispatched from Fort Rawlins in 1879 to support and safeguard the agent. They never got there. They were first met by a delegation of warriors under Chief Captain Jack, who reassured the soldiers that all was well and there was no threat to agent Meeker. The troops were then lured into a trap and fired on. More than half were slaughtered by the Utes, including the commanding officer.

Back at the Indian agency, Meeker made a fatal error. He plowed a new irrigation ditch across a racetrack cleared and graded by the Indians to race their prize horses. The enraged Indians killed all eleven men involved in the construction, including Meeker. Meeker's wife and his daughter, Josephine, convinced the warriors that it would be smarter to hold them as hostages rather than to kill them. Chief Douglas, according to legend, got very drunk after the massacre. He insisted that Josephine join him in a hymn sung over the stripped and mutilated body of her father. Douglas remembered many Christian hymns from a stint in a missionary school and sang them all, boasting to his captive about his fine singing voice.

The Ute chiefs requested a peace conference a month afterwards, at which they released their hostages as a gesture of goodwill. A craven federal bureaucrat decided that Meeker and his associates were not worth another Indian war. Very lenient terms were offered to the Utes. No attempt was made to punish those guilty of murder. No wonder that Meeker's ghost is still angry about this betrayal. It would be best to avoid being near the Meeker monument around dusk.

Ghosts of Climate Change

Some ghosts are scary. They inspire horror and fear in those who behold them. Other apparitions are so pathetic that they evoke more pity and sorrow in the hearts of the living than terror. The spirits of the cliff dwellers cause a reaction of sympathetic concern mixed with disbelief and surprise.

Mesa Verde National Park is one of the world's greatest archeological treasures, famed for its spectacular, well-preserved cliff dwellings. Southwestern Colorado's premier tourist attraction, Mesa Verde contains nearly five thousand archeological sites, including six hundred cliff dwellings. The largest, most splendid, and most photogenic cliff dwellings include Cliff Palace, Spruce Tree House, Square Tower House, and Sun Temple. Besides their fine stonework, these cliff dwellings have something else in common—ghosts.

For most observers, the phantom appearances are mercifully brief. An infant is glimpsed lying listlessly in a blanket. It is too weak to cry and too dehydrated to produce tears. Its skin is loose and crumpled in folds like the face of an English bulldog. The image dissolves in a whirl of dust. Another disturbing apparition, as reported by several tourists, is alleged to appear at Cliff Palace. The timing of these fleeting materializations seems to favor either the first or last tours of the day. The sun is relatively low in the sky, the shadows long and shifting quickly. Did they really see a man squatting in that doorway, witnesses ask themselves, or was it just a shifting shadow? The man is begging for water. His trembling hands hold up a pottery bowl. It is a beautifully decorated, very empty

bowl. His dry, crusty lips are seamed with cracks. Like the infant, his skin hangs loose, as though he has shrunken inside his skin. His hopeless lethargy is a sign that he has little time left in this existence. His skin color has an odd tint, evidence that his kidneys have ceased to function. Death by dehydration is an agonizingly slow and torturous process. The victim senses that the body is shutting down, function by function, organ by organ. The shadow of death is circling like a vulture, with each circle tighter and slower. These and the other ghosts said to haunt the cliff dwellings of Mesa Verde surely rank among the most heart-wrenching spirits ever witnessed by the living.

These are the ghosts of the ancient Pueblo people who built the cliff dwellings between about 900 and 1200 A.D. The dates are proven by studying the tree rings in the timbers that the Pueblos used in roofing their stone structures. These same tree rings also show that a great drought came to Mesa Verde in the year 1276 and persisted to 1299. The Pueblo people literally disappeared. They abandoned their homes and left in search of water. They were the victims of climate change.

Every living thing needs water—some more than others. The land that the Pueblo made their own was, at best, semidesert. Even a small decrease in annual rainfall would have been catastrophic. Rising temperatures could reduce the amount of water available to living things by increasing evaporation. Don't ask the ghosts of Mesa Verde if they believe in climate change. It's what killed them.

But what caused the climate change that doomed the cliff dwellers? Contemporary culprits—large human populations burning lots of fossil fuels—couldn't have contributed to climate change in the thirteenth century. The Ute, an unrelated tribe living in central and western Colorado, have an explanation in their ancient legends. The Ute interpretation of the Pueblo's fate blames the gods. Supposedly, the Pueblos once had been subterranean animals. They climbed up a magical cornstalk to the surface and became human. They displeased the gods by their arrogant behavior, and the gods withheld the vital rains.

Did the earth go through global warming more than seven centuries ago as part of a long-term climate cycle, or because of a supernatural curse on the Pueblo? Is the present global warming part of a long-term natural cycle, exacerbated by human activity, or is it a manifestation of the anger of the gods? The Pueblo might know.

The Opal Ring

Is it possible for an inanimate object—a piece of furniture, a decorative object, or a piece of jewelry—to have absorbed the spirit of a past owner? Some think so, and among the believers are members of a Grand Junction family. They have come to believe that an antique opal ring somehow contains the wisdom of its first owner, the grandmother of the ring's current owner.

Granny had been an interesting character, as her now elderly granddaughter remembered. In an era when middle-class women were expected to expend their energies and demonstrate their creativity in the domestic sphere only, she had been a very active and astute partner in her husband's business. Her husband was known to admit, following his two customary whiskeys after dinner, that she was "the real brains in the outfit." Her judgment was not perfect, but she made remarkably few errors in her business decisions.

In her old age, Granny had confided in her daughter that the source of her reputation for sound judgment was her opal ring. "When you have a problem to solve or a decision to make, look into the opal," she advised. "Stare down into its depths and ponder your problem or your question. The opal will lead you to the right answer. If the answer doesn't become obvious while you are meditating on the opal, keep it on when you go to bed. You'll have some interesting dreams." Granny also had another piece of advice regarding the ring: "Never sell the opal. Keep it in the family by passing it down to the eldest daughter."

The advice, like the ring itself, was dutifully passed on by the present owner's mother. Did the opal provide good advice? Was the semiprecious stone somehow channeling Granny's wisdom to her descendents? Or was there nothing special about the opal, and its "advice" just coincidental good luck?

"Tell me how it works," asked a family friend who was a psychologist. "Well, I look down into the stone, not just at it, if you know what I mean," the ring's owner explained. "I focus on the depths of the opal, down into the milky white matrix with its tiny iridescent points of color. It just kind of draws you in, then you begin thinking about your problem and, most of the time, the answer seems to form in your head. I'll give you an example.

"I was dating a guy I'll call Fred. He was great looking, outgoing, and ambitious. My girlfriends all were envious. The relationship was at the point where it was either going to move on to an official engagement or end. I remembered my mom's advice to think on it while focusing on the opal. The answer was to hold off for a while, give myself more time to think about it. I expected that Fred would be disappointed but understanding. He flew into a rage. It was frightening. I later found out he's already gone through two wives, both of whom alleged physical and psychological abuse. The opal ring warned me and I'm glad I listened."

"Don't you see what is happening has nothing to do with the supernatural?" asked the psychologist. "This is a classic example of self-hypnosis. You stare 'into' the opal as you say, putting yourself into a light trance. Your subconscious asserts itself, summarizing all the little clues you'd picked up about Fred's behavior and attitudes—things that seemed random and insignificant at the time but which formed a pattern when you looked at them again more critically."

"Okay, explain this," she replied. "Look at this opal. You see tiny planes of light, right? I can see your point about Fred—I already had the clues I needed to make the decision. But six months ago, I was scheduled to go on a little sightseeing flight with a friend of a friend who flew his own plane. When I woke up that morning and put the opal ring on, I noticed something really weird. The opal was actually blinking, like a neon sign winking on and off. The only color was red. I called the pilot and begged off, saying I said I had the flu. An hour later, I heard that the plane had crashed on takeoff. No one survived. How could I have known? The ring knew. Granny knew."

The psychologist had no answer for that. But he did buy his wife an opal ring. Do you have an opal ring yet?

The Worm Turns

The saga of old Uncle Charley, the worm who turned, has faded from the memories of most in the vicinity of Grand Junction. There was a time when children were disciplined by threatening them with a visit from Uncle Charley, or rather his vengeful spirit. Uncle Charley was a classic example of how unrelenting harassment can turn a mild-mannered, peaceable person into a violent engine of retaliation. He was the worm who turned, or, more accurately, the worm who returned from the dead.

Uncle Charley was an inoffensive old man living in evidently impoverished retirement in a small house on the town's outskirts. He wasn't anyone's uncle; rather, he was everybody's uncle, having been given that honorary title back when times were better for him and he was able to be a more generous neighbor. Time was when he had a smile for all and was an easy customer for Girl Scout cookies, school fundraiser candy bars, and so on.

Then tragedy struck. His beloved wife of many years died very slowly and painfully of cancer. Their health insurance company refused to pay her massive bills on the grounds that the treatment was experimental and thus not covered. Charley lost his wife, his life savings, and, possibly, his sanity. He retreated into the depths of his memories and became socially isolated. He stopped going to church, dropped out of clubs and organizations, and became an expert penny-pincher. He refused to answer the door at Halloween, or any other time, for that matter. He planted a large garden to reduce his food bills. He ignored the friendly greetings of neighbors and acquaintances.

Charley's habit of paying all bills, large and small, with cash started a rumor that he kept large sums of currency in his house or maybe buried in his garden. Adventurous young thugs began making late-night raids on Charley's garden, digging up and discarding immature root crops like beets and carrots, trampling his beans and tomatoes, and generally wreaking havoc. They just laughed at his feeble protests. When Charley went out to do his shopping, gangs of kids broke into his house and trashed it without discovering any cash. Things clearly were out of control. Then, suddenly, the worm turned.

A pair of delinquents sneaking into Charley's garden were confronted by a tall, shadowy figure who never made a sound but who hit them repeatedly and painfully with a garden rake. Bleeding heavily from multiple scrapes and punctures, they ran for their lives. That same evening, the gang's ringleader was attacked outside his own home. He was beaten with his own bat as he returned from baseball practice. Other veterans of past raids on Uncle Charley's property were similarly waylaid and brutally disciplined by the dark, silent figure, assumed to be that of Uncle Charley. A full week of vengeful punishment of the guilty went by. Finally, the parents of one boy, disbelieving his story of a schoolyard ruckus, got the true story and went to the police station to file a complaint against Uncle Charley. The astonished police sergeant told them it was too late to pursue Uncle Charley—he'd been found dead of a heart attack on a downtown street a week earlier.

All Aboard!

He doesn't always show up, which is fair enough, as he is not on salary. In fact, he's never there in a real sense, as he is only a ghost. Have no fear. He is not an evil, intrusive, or scary ghost—quite the opposite. Most people who've witnessed his brief appearances had no idea that they'd seen a ghost. He plays his role to perfection, and with evident pride in his job. The phantom may simply be continuing the job he held in life, or he could be fulfilling a fantasy of working on the railroad—a dream of many American boys who grew up in the golden age of steam locomotives.

"All aboard! All aboard now!" the man or rather, his spirit, loves to shout as the train departs the station. Clearly, he has a flair for the dramatic. The figure is that of an elderly, somewhat portly man. His handsome, flushed face is distinguished by a neatly trimmed mustache of pure white, matching his hair. His dark blue uniform is piped in bright yellow, matching the color of the antique passenger cars. The phantom is playing the role of a conductor on one of the most famous antique trains in the country. The Durango and Silverton Rail Line has been in continuous operation since 1881, and hasn't changed much in appearance. The ghost matches the vintage equipment and, who knows, might be just as old as the coal-fired steam locomotives.

The phantom conductor likes to do what the other, living conductors call "walk-throughs," leisurely strolls through the cars to check that all is well with the passengers. "Are you comfortable?" he'll ask. "Are you enjoying the ride?" Recently, an unsuspecting tourist couple from New Jersey asked him to pose for a picture with them. Later, when they looked at the day's photos on their computer screen, they saw that, while their likenesses were sharp and clear, the figure of the conductor was faint and fuzzy, as though out of focus.

The ghost never appears in the same car as railroad employees. He has never been known to frighten anyone. His evident pleasure in the scenery and in the whole ambiance of the beautifully maintained antique train contributes to the passengers' enjoyment. In his smiling way, the spirit of the ghost conductor personifies the adventurous spirit of the Old West.

Butch and Sundance Ride Again

These phantoms not only appear sporadically and unpredictably, but they switch clothing as well, at least according to reported sightings. To some, the apparitions gradually materialize out of dust caught up in the miniature whirlwinds known as dust devils. They take form as two men on horseback, dressed as late-nineteenth-century cowboys. Both wear twin revolvers and cartridge belts. They are at ease in the saddle and at ease with one another—old friends with shared interests and skills. Both are handsome men; the stockier of the two wears a mustache and an infectious grin. Other observers have seen the same two men on foot and dressed elegantly in tailored three-piece suits, complete with gold watch chains stretched across the vests. The mustached one wears a handsome gray derby. They look like bankers, which in a way they are, though they only make withdrawals. Meet the ghosts of two of the American West's most famous nineteenth-century desperados: Butch Cassidy and the Sundance Kid.

Butch and Sundance became legends in their own time for several reasons, not the least of which was their professional prowess. They raised robbing banks to an art. Butch had a flair for image-shaping. He saw that fostering a reputation as the "Robin Hood of the West" would dampen folks' enthusiasm for informing law officers about his whereabouts and habits. He took pains not to kill anyone if he could avoid it, and seldom stole personal possessions like jewelry.

Butch's favorite haunt in Colorado was the, dry, remote, almost-empty northwestern corner of the state. It was his refuge from the law as a living man, and it's his favorite place as a ghost. Brown's Park, also called Brown's Hole, is a nearly flat valley at the northern end of Dinosaur National Monument. This desolate, isolated area was a near-perfect hideout for Butch and the "wild bunch," as he called the gang he organized in 1896. The area is famous for its large number of fossilized dinosaur bones. In a way, Butch and Sundance were dinosaurs of a different sort. They became glamorized folk heroes because they were among the last of a dying breed: the fast-riding, jauntily independent adventurer-outlaw of the Old West. By Butch and Sundance's time, the 1880s and 1890s, the west was being tamed, for better or for worse. Railroads were changing the economic and cultural landscapes in dramatic ways.

Butch was born William Leroy Parker, the first of thirteen children of a hardworking, churchgoing Utah family. By the time he was twenty-three, he had learned cattle rustling from his mentor in crime, Mike Cassidy, whom he honored by taking his last name. "Butch" sounded more macho than Bill or Leroy, and so Butch Cassidy was created. Butch's first bank robbery took place in Telluride. He and his gang were soon robbing banks in Utah, Idaho, Montana, and Nevada as well as Colorado. Butch could be a charmer; his broad smile and easygoing manner were perfectly portrayed by Paul Newman in the classic 1969 film, *Butch Cassidy and the Sundance Kid*. His penchant for robbing trains added to his growing reputation as a Robin Hood. Many people at the time resented the enormous power of the railroads over all aspects of the economy. Ranching, farming, and mining all depended on the railroads. Everything, including money, traveled by train, and Butch decided that trains were almost as good as banks as sources of easy money. To many otherwise law-abiding citizens, robbing the Union Pacific railroad was not an outrage, it was revenge for the UP's high-handed and ruthless manipulations of freight rates and state legislatures. Harassing the Union Pacific added to the Robin Hood myth that Butch consciously encouraged.

So there they are, the ghosts of two folk heroes, riding boldly across the lonely expanses of what is now Brown's Park National Wildlife Refuge. It is fitting that the phantom leaders of the "wild bunch" should materialize in a wildlife refuge, a place that preserves a chunk of the old Wild West that Butch and Sundance strived to personify.

Tastes Like Pork

"Tastes just like pork," he'd say, flashing an evil grin. "Yessir, just like roast pork. Best with fresh garlic, or so I've heard, not that I'd know," deftly adding a denial.

Alfred Packer was a wily one all right, and had the devil's own luck, for in his case, the judicial system failed miserably. He got away with murder, and worse, he was an unrepentant cannibal. His annoyingly smug and boastful ghost is said to appear regularly in remote sections of Hinsdale County. Actually, all of Hinsdale County could be considered remote, as the population of the entire county is less than a thousand. And its county seat, Lake City, holds but a few hundred souls. Those living inhabitants are wary of meeting the smirking ghost of Alfred Packer. He got away with it, everyone knew he got away with it, and nobody can do anything about it, especially now that he is Colorado's most self-satisfied, arrogant, and downright evil ghost. The only good news about Packer's ghost is that it seems to stay in Hinsdale County, which may be the emptiest county in America. The odds of encountering this ghost are, geographically speaking, remote.

In December of 1873 a large party of gold prospectors from Utah reached the camp of Ouray, the great chief of the Utes and a friend to whites who came in peace. Ouray urged the men to stay in his camp until spring, advising them that winter on the continental divide was not to be taken lightly. Some heeded his warning but six decided to move on, blinded by the glitter of the gold that was rumored to be in the rugged mountains to the east. Six weeks later, Packer alone appeared at the Los Pinos Indian Agency near Gunnison, claiming that he had been abandoned by his companions and forced to live off wild roots and berries. His story made no sense, as he was plump in appearance and his first request was for whiskey, not food. He claimed to have no money, but a few days later he was buying drinks for all in a bar in Lake City.

Later in the summer of 1874, a party of the Utes on a hunting expedition stumbled on the mutilated bodies of five men half hidden in a snow bank near Lake City. Their skulls had been crushed and, horrifically, they had been butchered like hogs. The flesh had been stripped from their thighs and calves, and the flesh of their stomach muscles was gone. The clean cuts suggested a knife, not the teeth of wild animals. One observer commented that, if the carcasses had been hogs and not men, it would have looked like someone took the most desirable cuts: the hams and bellies, or bacon.

Packer was arrested on suspicion of murder but managed to escape from jail. In 1883, he was recaptured in Wyoming and returned to Lake City for trial. He was found guilty and sentenced to hang by an irate judge who shouted at Packer that he had "eaten half the Democrats in Hinsdale County and deserved to hang." An appeals court overturned the death penalty on the grounds that the trial was held in an atmosphere poisoned by unsubstantiated rumors of cannibalism. In 1886, Packer was found guilty at a second trial and sentenced to forty years in prison for manslaughter. He was paroled in 1901.

To his astonished delight, Packer discovered that his reputation as a cannibal made him a kind of perverse celebrity. Saloon patrons would buy him drinks to hear him expound on recipes for human flesh consumption. His listeners seemed to get a weird thrill from rubbing elbows with such pure evil contained in such an ordinary body. It seems unbelievable that a man could commit such a gross offense as murdering and eating his companions and yet show no remorse at all. Meeting Packer's ghost would be like having a quick tour of the depths of hell. Think twice before buying a drink for a gracious old-timer in a bar in Hinsdale County, unless you want to hear a ghostly reminiscence of murder and cannibalism, that is. Are you up for a gruesome tale?

Legend of the White Burro

The family of tourists from New York had had a long day. They were on the scenic highway from Aspen, heading for Glenwood Springs, where they had promised themselves a long, refreshing soak in the famous hot springs. Aspen had been a highlight of their Colorado vacation, which would end all too soon. They were about to travel a portion of the highway that entered a winding, descending curve when the driver suddenly slammed on the brakes. There in the middle of the road stood a white burro. There was, fortunately for everyone, no other traffic at the moment.

Tires screeching, the car shuddered to a halt inches in front of the creature, which stared at the family calmly. Tossing its head, the animal gave its distinctive bray, a sound that has been likened to a very rusty chainsaw cutting through a knotty log, but without the lulling melody.

The white burro slowly ambled its way across the highway and then disappeared in the roadside vegetation. In an instant, it was gone. At that precise moment, the family heard a loud rumbling sound just around the bend in the road. The ground shook and a cloud of dust rose. They cautiously drove around the curve to find a huge pile of boulders blocking their path. A massive landslide covered the pavement. If the white burro had not appeared when and where it did, they would have been killed. Badly shaken, they continued on their way and reached their motel without any further incident.

At dinner, their waitress overheard them discussing their experience that evening over a leisurely dinner. "You saw a burro—a white burro—just before the landslide ahead?" she queried. "Are you sure it was white?" After hearing the whole story, the waitress told them that they had seen a legend.

Burros were essential in the settlement of Colorado and much of the west. Burros and mining went together. The animals were incredibly strong for their size, able to carry heavy loads on steep slopes. Large ears and sensitive noses helped them locate running water, and they could eat almost anything. They were intelligent and, most of the time, friendly to people. On occasion, they could be stubborn and perverse, but mostly they were loyal workmates and companions. Their raucous brays led to their nicknames: "Rocky Mountain Canary" and "Colorado Mockingbird."

The supportive dispositions of the friendly little beasts contributed to the legend of the white burro as a supernatural protector of people in danger throughout the Rocky Mountains. The story was that a phantom white burro would appear mysteriously across the path of people unknowingly headed for disaster. The white burro warned of imminent danger; after doing his duty, the apparition would disappear. Ignoring the white burro would be a fatal error, so watch carefully for one while in the Rocky Mountains. And listen for the song of the Colorado Mockingbird.

The Spirit Twin

Nancy always wondered what it would have been like to grow up with a twin. She thought that life would have been far different if she had shared it with a sister. Not that she had a bad life—far from it—but a close companion would have been a blessing. Since she had been old enough to understand, Nancy had known that she had shared the womb with a twin who did not survive the trauma of birth. Poor little Margaret lived less than an hour. It had become a family tradition to visit Margaret's grave on her birthday—the birthday she shared, of course, with Nancy. As Nancy grew up, her parents repeatedly asked if she might prefer to shift the annual cemetery visit to another date. Nancy, however, sensed that her birthday was shadowed by those early-morning visits with her twin. Margaret's spirit, her twin believed, appreciated her family's thoughtfulness, and Nancy felt that her connection to Margaret was strengthened in some way too.

Nancy was the only child of a prosperous Grand Junction businessman and his devoted wife, who was able to be a stay-at-home mom. Love and attention were as abundant as material possessions. Life was good, all the more so because Margaret was with Nancy in spirit. Nancy and Margaret had a continuous, if unspoken, dialogue going. Never knowing any alternative experience, Nancy accepted this spiritual communication as completely normal.

She was six years old when Margaret's spirit saved her life the first time. Nancy was walking to school and was not focused on her surroundings, oblivious to the heavy traffic around her. As luck would have it, the elderly crossing guard who manned the busy intersection across from the school was absent that day. Nancy waited patiently for the light to turn green and was about to step off the curb. "No!" was shouted in her ear so loudly that Nancy jumped straight up in the air, or so she remembered later. Safe on the sidewalk, she felt the hot breeze as a large truck careened around the corner, missing her by inches. Without the shouted warning, Nancy surely would have been killed. But who had yelled "no"? Some classmates who witnessed the event believed that Nancy herself had said it, but Nancy of course knew better. It had been Margaret's spirit who saved her.

A few years later, Nancy's parents took her to a traveling carnival. Nancy was waiting in line with playmates for a ride on the big Ferris wheel, happy that she had persuaded her parents that she was tall enough to ride without a parent alongside. As the line inched along, Nancy suddenly had the sensation that someone, or something, was holding her back. Her feet seemed glued to the ground. Her face turned white and she clung to a fence for support. Her parents, thinking that she had had too much sun, took her back to the car. As she sat there drinking a cold soda, they were startled to hear screams of terror. The rusted bolts holding the spokes of the giant wheel to the hub had failed under stress and allowed the seats currently at the top to topple over. Eight passengers were injured as they fell forty feet to hard-packed earth. Had Margaret intervened again? Nancy was sure that was what had happened, and equally sure that she should not try to explain this spiritual protector's role in her narrow escapes. She didn't want people to look at her strangely.

Another memorable instance of her twin fending off danger took place when Nancy was a young adult, busy building her career. She was scheduled to fly to Denver, connecting there to a flight to New York for an important conference. She would have to be at the airport at seven in the morning, so she set two alarm clocks. She awakened at 6:30 to find that both alarms had been mysteriously placed in the spare bedroom—under pillows and turned off. Could she have done this herself, reacting to a subconscious demand from her guardian twin spirit? Nancy had little time to ponder that. Turning on the television as she fixed breakfast, she learned about the disaster at the airport. The plane for which she had a ticket had crashed on takeoff. There were no survivors.

Nancy continues the tradition of visiting Margaret's grave on their birthday. She bows her head in gratitude for her guardian spirit. Her twin will always be with her.

Bibliography

American Automobile Association. *Colorado and Utah Tour Book*. Heathrow, FL: AAA Publishing, 2010.

Baker, M., and Leroy Hafen. *History of Colorado*. Denver: State Historical Society of Colorado, 1927.

Beckley, Timothy. *The UFO Silencers*. New Brunswick, NJ: Inner Light, 1990.

Botkin, B. A., ed. *A Treasury of American Folklore*. New York: Crown Publishers, 1944.

———. *A Treasury of Western Folklore*. New York: Crown Publishers, 1951.

Breakenridge, William. *Helldorado*. Boston: Houghton Mifflin, 1928.

Clark, Jerome. *Unexplained!* Canton, MI: Visible Ink Press, 1999.

Coleman, Loren. *Mysterious America*. London: Faber and Faber, 1983.

Colorado Writers Project of the Works Project Administration. *Colorado: A Guide to the Highest State*. New York: Hastings House, 1941.

Daegling, David. *Bigfoot Exposed*. Walnut Creek, CA: AltaMira Press, 2004.

Dorson, Richard. *American Folklore*. Chicago: University of Chicago Press, 1959.

Epting, Chris. *The Birthplace Book: A Guide to Birth Sites of Famous People, Places and Things*. Mechanicsburg, PA: Stackpole Books, 2009.

Green, John. *Encounters with Bigfoot*. Surrey, BC: Hancock House, 1994.

Guiley, Rosemary. *The Encyclopedia of Ghosts and Spirits*. New York: Facts on File, 1992.

Harper, Charles. Haunted Houses: *Tales of the Supernatural*. Philadelphia: J. B. Lippincott, 1930.

Hauck, Dennis. *Haunted Places: The National Directory*. New York: Penguin-Putnam, 2002.

Krantz, Grover. *Bigfoot/Sasquatch Evidence*. Surrey, BC: Hancock House, 1999.

Krantz, Les. *America by the Numbers: Facts and Figures from the Weighty to the Way-Out*. Boston: Houghton Mifflin, 1993.

Mack, John. *Abduction: Human Encounters with Aliens*. New York: Scribners, 1994.

Myers, Arthur. *A Ghost Hunter's Guide to Haunted Landmarks, Parks, Churches and Other Public Places*. Chicago: Contemporary Books, 1993.

——. *The Ghostly Register*. New York: McGraw-Hill/Contemporary Books, 1986.

Norman, Michael, and Beth Scott. *Historic Haunted America*. New York: Tor, 1995.

Pickering, David. *Casell Dictionary of Superstitions*. London: Casell, 1995.

Skinner, Charles. *American Myths and Legends*. Detroit: Gale Research Co., 1974.

Stein, George, ed. *The Encyclopedia of the Paranormal*. Buffalo, NY: Prometheus, 1996.

Taylor, Troy. *The Haunting of America: Ghosts and Legends from America's Past*. Alton, IL: Whitechapel Productions, 2001.

Thompson, C. J. S. *The Mystery and Lore of Apparitions*. London: Harold Shaylor, 1930.

Websites

ghosteyes.com
AmericanFolklore.net
LegendsofAmerica.com
TheShadowLands.net/places/Colorado.html

Acknowledgments

THIS IS MY TWELFTH BOOK WRITTEN UNDER THE SKILLFUL GUIDANCE AND friendly counsel of my editor, Kyle Weaver. Assistant editor Brett Keener shepherded the manuscript through production with his usual professional efficiency and sensitivity. Artist Marc Radle created the haunting illustrations.

Steve Eckardt kept my computer healthy and obedient. Elizabeth Eckardt produced a coherent manuscript from my sloppy handwriting. They have my heartfelt thanks.

My first visit to Colorado was on a "family field trip" that included Colorado Springs, Rocky Mountain National Park, Steamboat Springs, Mesa Verde, and Durango. Good friends and fellow geographers Chet and Chesha Zimolzak accompanied me in exploring Denver, Garden of the Gods, and Royal Gorge.

I appreciate the friendly and efficient assistance of the professional librarians at the McCowan Library in Pitman, the Gloucester County Library, and Campbell Library at Rowan University. My good friend Herb Richardson helped locate source materials.

My dear wife Diane lovingly accepted the more or less permanent presence of my untidy stacks of books, maps, and papers in the charming home she has made beautiful by her presence and love. Thanks again to my darling soulmate. You have all my love always.

About the Author

CHARLES A. STANSFIELD JR. TAUGHT GEOGRAPHY AT ROWAN UNIVERSITY in Glassboro, New Jersey, for forty-one years and published fifteen textbooks on cultural and regional geography. In the course of his research, he realized that stories of ghosts and other strange phenomena reflect the history, culture, economy, and even physical geography of a region, leading him to collect tales from all parts of the country. He is the author of *Haunted Presidents* and nine other titles in the Stackpole Books Haunted Series: *Haunted Washington, Haunted Arizona, Haunted Northern California, Haunted Southern California, Haunted Ohio, Haunted Vermont, Haunted Maine, Haunted Jersey Shore,* and *Haunted New Jersey*.

Other Titles in the
Haunted Series